ATHENAGORAS

EMBASSY FOR THE CHRISTIANS
THE RESURRECTION OF THE DEAD

ΠΡΕϹΒΕΙΑ ΠΕΡΙ ΧΡΙϹΤΙΑΝΩΝ
ΠΕΡΙ ΑΝΑϹΤΑϹΕΩϹ ΝΕΚΡΩΝ

ANCIENT CHRISTIAN WRITERS

THE WORKS OF THE FATHERS IN TRANSLATION

EDITED BY

JOHANNES QUASTEN, S. T. D.
Catholic University of America
Washington, D.C.

JOSEPH C. PLUMPE, Ph.D.
Pontifical College Josephinum
Worthington, O.

No. 23

ATHENAGORAS

EMBASSY FOR THE CHRISTIANS
THE RESURRECTION OF
THE DEAD

TRANSLATED AND ANNOTATED

BY

JOSEPH HUGH CREHAN, S.J.

Professor of Theology
Heythrop College, Oxon

NEWMAN PRESS

New York, N.Y./Ramsey, N.J.

De Licentia Superioris S.J.
  Nihil Obstat
      J. Quasten
        Cens. Dep.

Imprimatur:
      Patricius A. O'Boyle, D.D.
        Archiep. Washingtonen.
          die 5 Nov. 1955

Library of Congress
Catalog Card Number: 56-11421

ISBN: 0-8091-0036-3

PUBLISHED BY PAULIST PRESS
Editorial Office: 1865 Broadway, New York, N.Y. 10023
Business Office: 545 Island Road, Ramsey, N.J. 07446

PRINTED AND BOUND IN THE UNITED STATES OF AMERICA

CONTENTS

ATHENAGORAS

EMBASSY FOR THE CHRISTIANS
THE RESURRECTION OF THE DEAD

ΠΡΕϹΒΕΙΑ ΠΕΡΙ ΧΡΙϹΤΙΑΝΩΝ

ΠΕΡΙ ΑΝΑϹΤΑϹΕΩϹ ΝΕΚΡΩΝ

INTRODUCTION

When the emperor Domitian sent for the surviving 'brethren of the Lord' from Palestine, and having examined them about their descent from David dismissed them in peace, the age of the Apologies may be said to have begun. To all Christians it had been made clear that if they could gain access to the emperor, even to the most erratic and cruel of emperors, and state their case to him, there would be a very good chance of justice being done to them. From this episode and from the wider activities of the emperor Hadrian, who travelled much in the eastern part of his empire, the Christians gathered courage to come forward with answers to the odious calumnies of child murder and cannibalism, of incest and atheism, which a paganism, sometimes interested and sometimes uncomprehending, levelled against them.

The work of apologizing thus for Christianity was undertaken for the most part by laymen; it was not part of the official preaching of the Church. Quite apart from its effect on the pagans to whom it might, or might not, be delivered, it had the effect of supplying less educated and less experienced Christians with arguments to use when they might chance to be themselves put upon their trial in a moment of persecution. Thus one finds that the work of Athenagoras carries arguments and turns of phrase which appear again in the *Acts* of the martyr Apollonius who was put to death in Rome by Commodus in A.D. 185. One cannot claim a direct literary dependence between the two works, but it is clear from them that

3

these ideas were 'in the air' and formed part of a common stock of Christian apologetic at the time. Athenagoras is perhaps distinguished among the apologists in his gentlemanly tone and by his coming to closer grips with Greek religion and philosophy than was usual in a Christian.

THE LIFE OF ATHENAGORAS

The only facts recorded in ancient times about Athenagoras are contained in a small fragment of Philip of Side's *Christian History* which was first printed by Dodwell in 1689 and which has been reprinted in Migne.[1] The fragment was copied by Dodwell (from Cod. Barocc. 142) in the Bodleian Library and ascribed by him to Nicephorus Callistus or to some other late Greek historian who had made excerpts from Philip of Side and others. It reads:

> Philip of Side says in his twenty-fourth book: Athenagoras was the first director of the School at Alexandria; his *floruit* was about the time of Hadrian and Antoninus, to whom he dedicated his *Embassy* on behalf of the Christians. He was a man who professed Christianity while still wearing the philosopher's garb and was the leading man in the Academic School. Before Celsus he had planned to write against the Christians, but, reading the Holy Scriptures to make his attack the more telling, he was so won over by the Holy Spirit as to become, like the great Paul, a teacher and not a persecutor of the faith he was attacking. Philip says that Clement, author of the *Stromata*, was his disciple and Pantaenus Clement's. Pantaenus too was an Athenian, being a Pythagorean in his philosophy.

The extract goes on to enumerate the heads of the Catechetical School of Alexandria down to Rhodon, who

moved the School to Philip's own town of Side in Pam-
phylia in the time of Theodosius the Great, where Philip
himself attended it. The dating of Athenagoras to the time
of Hadrian and Antoninus is an obvious mistake, based
perhaps on a misreading of the title at the head of his
Embassy. The full name of Marcus Aurelius there inscribed
was Marcus Aurelius Antoninus, and it is notorious how
easily such lists of names acquired additions in ancient
MSS. The case of the *Apology* of Aristides may be cited.
That the *Embassy* cannot be from the time of Hadrian is
shown by the reference in ch. 30 to the deification of
Hadrian's favourite Antinous, an act that is ascribed there to
'your ancestors.' Much has been made of the discrepancy
between Philip of Side and Eusebius over the succession
to Athenagoras. Eusebius makes the succession go from
Pantaenus through Clement to Origen. In one place he
says explicitly that Clement succeeded Pantaenus, but his
earlier and more detailed account reads as if he thought
that Pantaenus after one spell as head of the School went
as a missionary towards India, and on his return resumed
the headship which he had entrusted to Clement in his
absence. Certainly Alexander of Jerusalem, whose letter
to his friend Origen is quoted by Eusebius, speaks of
Pantaenus and Clement as if they were both known to
Origen and had been his masters.[2] From the dating of
Origen's career, it is hard to suppose that he had been a
disciple of Pantaenus before the start of the missionary
enterprise towards India. All told, then, it would seem
that Philip's account of the early days of the School of
Alexandria is not so wildly inaccurate as many have
supposed. At all events, as I have argued elsewhere[3]:

> Philip, however much he may have merited the strictures of
> his rival church-historian Socrates (7.27) for the rest of his work,

is here in a position to speak from knowledge. The catechetical school had continued at Alexandria until Philip's own day, and he had attended it. In his time, and perhaps through his instrumentality, the school was transferred to Side, his native place, where it soon died a natural death. Clearly Philip is a more important witness on the subject of this school than on matters of Church history. In a parallel way, it might be said, there are a number of members of Balliol College whose statements on Scottish history might not be trustworthy, but who could give, in a paragraph, quite an intelligible account of the person of John Balliol.

Dodwell (506) argues for the same solution at some length, and his reasons have never been satisfactorily answered.

The principal MS of Athenagoras[4] describes him in its title as an Athenian and a Christian philosopher. That an Athenian and a foreigner should be head of the School of Alexandria need occasion no surprise, for Pantaenus too was in all probability a Sicilian, being referred to affectionately by Clement[5] as the 'Sicilian bee.' In the same passage Clement lists his other teachers, among whom the first is an Ionian whom he met in Athens. Tollinton is not adverse to Zahn's suggestion that this Ionian at Athens was Athenagoras, but, as Clement is praising his teachers for their unwritten teaching as distinct from written books, it is hardly likely that he includes such a writer as Athenagoras in his list. It is also doubtful whether Clement, who was not a native of Alexandria, arrived there in time to enjoy the teaching of Athenagoras, who must be supposed to have died soon after A.D. 180.

There are plenty of signs, in the form of borrowings of technical terms and use of identical quotations from the classics, to show that Clement was indebted to the writings of Athenagoras, even though the carefully compiled index of Stählin gives no instance where Clement has reproduced verbatim a passage from Athenagoras. Clement was himself an eclectic in philosophy,[6] but his master Pantaenus was if anything a Stoic. Clement tried to pick the best from Stoicism and from the Platonic system, and it looks very much as if he owed much of his Platonic borrowings to Athenagoras. There can be little doubt in the mind of anyone who reads through Athenagoras that he was well versed in Platonism, and there is a strong probability that he was the Athenagoras to whom, as Photius tells us,[7] Boethus dedicated a book on *Difficult Sentences in Plato*. Photius has occasion to mention our Athenagoras elsewhere in his work and does so without giving him any qualifying title. The inference therefore is that when he refers to an Athenagoras again in the same work, he means the same person. If this inference is correct, it gives further point to the statement of Philip of Side that Athenagoras was a leading man in the Platonic school at Alexandria.

Methodius of Olympus, who was martyred in 311, is the first and almost the only patristic writer to quote Athenagoras's work. Writing on the Resurrection, he must naturally have turned to the similar work of a fellow Platonist. In five or six places he shows dependence upon the *Embassy*, though only once does he refer to Athenagoras by name.[8] Epiphanius and Photius have used this passage of Methodius and recall the name of Athenagoras, but, these apart, there is no mention of him in the whole of antiquity. The complete neglect of so accomplished a piece of work as the *Resurrection* is very surprising, and would inevitably raise the question whether the work might not be a later composition of an unknown author, if it were not for the internal evidence. In ch. 36 of the *Embassy* Athenagoras deliberately sets aside the theme of the bodily resurrection for another occasion, though it was part of the stock material of the Apologists,[9] and might be expected in an address to the emperor on Christianity. In the *Resurrection*, ch. 8, Athenagoras has apparently borrowed some of Tatian's ideas, and throughout this work the diction is exactly that of the writer of the *Embassy*, with the sole difference that as the *Resurrection* is a public lecture, a more formal tone has crept in here and there. Thus I notice that the adjective ἀνθρωπικός which is used for 'human' exclusively in the *Embassy*, never appears in the *Resurrection*, where it is replaced by ἀνθρώπινος or ἀνθρώπειος. Anyone who has worked through Schwartz's *Index verborum* will remain fully convinced that the two works are by the same writer. Added to this is the testimony of the principal MS, compiled at a time when 5th-century MSS were being copied in the scriptoria of Byzantium.

There is one small piece of evidence which points to Alexandria as the place of origin of the *Resurrection*. In ch. 12 when Athenagoras is enumerating, by way of illustration, the buildings a farmer has to set up, he includes a shelter for his camels. Now no Athenian or Western Greek, and indeed no Greek of the province of Asia, would be so familiar with the presence of camels in his everyday experience as to include them in a casual illustration of this kind. But an Egyptian Greek would. So would a Syrian Greek; but no one has ever suggested that Athenagoras was connected with Syria. In Egypt the camel was regularly used in the postal service; [10] Syria was its home; while the only camels brought to Greece were those which came in Xerxes's army, most of which were devoured by lions on the way.

The accusation of Montanism has been brought against

Athenagoras, not by his contemporaries, but by post-Reformation scholars, who were answered by Maranus in his edition.[11] The charge is based on a similarity of phrase between *Embassy* 9 (where the image of the flute-player and the flute is used to illustrate prophetic inspiration) and some words of Montanus preserved by Epiphanius, where the image is that of the lyre. The fact is that the image is drawn from common stock, occurring also in Hippolytus, Justin, Pseudo-Justin, Tertullian, and Philo, and ultimately coming from Plato.[12] The other ground for the charge was the strange view of second marriages taken by Athenagoras.[13] But, as J. P. Arendzen remarked,[14] if Athenagoras had been a Montanist, he would not have been content to call second marriage *covert* adultery or *fair-seeming*, but would have condemned it outright. Athenagoras was one of those who took very much to heart the words of Christ in the gospel about what God had joined together. Hermas[15] represents himself as being in doubt whether a widow's remarriage is sinful and professes to have had assurance from the Lord that it was not, but that continence would be much more praiseworthy. Such an episode shows that two opposite tendencies were at work among Christians of the 2nd century; the tendency which Athenagoras followed in this matter may have led others into Montanism, but he must be said to have stopped short of it, for the reason given above.

The *True Discourse* of Celsus the Platonist was written about the year 178, and hence Philip of Side is right in placing the conversion of Athenagoras some time before that year, for the date of the *Embassy* must fall somewhere between 176 and 180. L. Aurelius Commodus became associated with his father M. Aurelius as emperor on Nov.

27, 176, and Marcus himself died on Mar. 17, 180. As
both of these are called emperors in the title of the work,
it must naturally have been composed between the two
dates. A difficulty was raised by Mommsen about the
title 'Armenian victors' which occurs along with other
honorific titles in the dedication of the work.[16] Mommsen
thought that this title had never been awarded to Commodus, though allowed that it had been borne by L.
Verus along with Marcus until the death of L. Verus in
169. He therefore proposed to change the text to
'German victors,' as this title could be allowed to M.
Aurelius and Commodus. Geffcken accepted Mommsen's
arguments, but did not alter the text, claiming instead
that the whole dedication was probably spurious. Since
Mommsen's day the evidence of papyri and inscriptions
has piled up to show that M. Aurelius and Commodus
did jointly use the title of Armenian victor,[17] while other
documents show (what Mommsen denied) that Com-
modus continued to use this title after the death of Marcus
in 180. Indeed the uniform practice in these documents
seems to be to enumerate the imperial titles in this order:
Armenian, Median, Parthian, German, Sarmatian victor.
Athenagoras, by giving the first and the last of these, will
thus in all probability have been abbreviating a well-
known list by giving its first and last members.[18] Having
thus seen reason to reject the excessive scepticism with
which these German scholars handled this dedication, we
shall be able to view their later efforts at alteration of the
text with more detachment. Further to determine the
date of the *Embassy* within the period 176–180 by finding
a suitable time for the 'profound peace' mentioned in
ch. 1 does not seem possible. The idea is a rhetorical
commonplace in many classical speeches—even in Paul's

speech before Felix—and need not be supposed to point
to a short interval in 177 when Marcus was able to pause
between two great military tasks. That Christians were
accused of cannibalism by their slaves in Lyons in 177,
while Athenagoras (*Emb.* 35) says this has never happened,
hardly gives us a *terminus ante quem*. He may not have heard
of the event.

Analysis of the 'Embassy'

1-2 EXORDIUM: In a time of generally just rule, Christians
cannot be at peace for all their devout worship of God;
they are persecuted for their Name and refused the
justice that is not denied to criminals.

3 PLAN OF SPEECH: The charges are atheism, cannibalism,
and promiscuity.

REPLY TO FIRST CHARGE:

4 Christians believe in one God.

5-6 Poets and philosophers such as Plato said the same
and were not considered atheists.

7 They were guessing, but Christians draw their knowledge from the prophets.

8 Suppose there were a multitude of gods; it would
lead to many absurdities,

9 whereas Christians rely on writings inspired by the
Spirit of God.

10 Christians worship the Son and the Spirit along with
the Father.

11-12 They believe in angels and live useful lives so as
to be above suspicion of atheism.

13 FIRST OBJECTION COUNTERED: Even though we do not
sacrifice, that does not make us atheists,

2

14 nor does our lack of reverence for the gods of each city, for these differ from place to place and the men of one city are atheist in respect of the gods of another city.

15 Even if all agreed about gods, the Christians would be superior, for our God is not material,

16 nor is He the universe, but its Maker,

17 nor of recent human creation like the statues of the gods.

18 SECOND OBJECTION COUNTERED: But many say that they do not worship the statues of the gods. Let me tell you of the origin of those gods.

19 These transient beings cannot be gods,

20 nor can beings with bodies and bodily passions,

21 nor beings that weep and grow angry and lecherous,

22 nor can one allegorize such tales of the gods in terms of the elements.

23 THIRD OBJECTION COUNTERED: But do not some statues act and show power? This is devil's work,

24 for devils exist, being fallen angels,

25 and work through the statues of false gods,

26 as can be proved by the worship they require,

27 which is procured by the influence they have on men's imagination.

28 These gods have all been men once, as Herodotus and others show;

29 and they lived and died as men do.

30 Either the poets, who have won them worship, are lying; or these tales of gods fighting and dying are true, and the gods mortal.

REPLY TO SECOND CHARGE:

31 We cannot be cannibals, for we believe that God sees all we do and will reward or punish us.

REPLY TO THIRD CHARGE:

32 The stories of our promiscuity are merely the imputa-
tions of those who desire it for themselves and see it
in their gods.

33 We believe that the unity of the flesh is for the pro-
pagating of children.

34 Your governors find it hard to restrain the immorality
that prevails, but we have the strictest laws.

35 We could not be cannibals without murder, and yet
we will not countenance gladiators or abortion.

36 We believe in a resurrection. This may be folly, but
it is not a source of wickedness.

37 CONCLUSION: We pray for Your Majesties and obey
your laws.

ANALYSIS OF THE 'RESURRECTION'

1 EXORDIUM: Difficulties must first be removed before
the positive arguments can be given.

2 The objections are either that God cannot or that He
will not do it. If He cannot, this is either from lack of
knowledge or of power.

3 FIRST OBJECTION COUNTERED: But God knows how to
create and the work of restoration requires no more
power than creation.

4 SECOND OBJECTION COUNTERED: But what if a man is
eaten by beasts which then become the food of another
man?

5 God has assigned to each animal its proper food.

6 What is not natural food will not be incorporated into
the animal's flesh.

7 But even if it was incorporated, it would not stay there
for ever.

8 Unless it can be shown that cannibalism is natural, no objection lies.

9 The analogy with the potter, who cannot remake broken pots, is not exact.

10 THIRD OBJECTION COUNTERED: If God was unwilling, this would be either because it was unjust or unbecoming to Himself. But neither is the case.

11 RECAPITULATION: The discourse for the truth and that about the truth.

12–13 ARGUMENT FROM CREATION AND ITS MOTIVE: Man was created in the image of God, to know Him and to remain for ever. Hence God will not destroy him.

14 ARGUMENT FROM THE NATURE OF MAN (this argument is prior to that from rewards and penalties):

15 Man is soul and body. Soul alone, or body alone, is incomplete.

16 Sleep and death break this completeness, but interruption is not dissolution.

17 Begetting and growth are so wonderful that the restitution of the body is quite credible.

18 ARGUMENT FROM REWARDS AND PENALTIES: It is unjust to reward or to punish the soul alone.

19–20 In case God's providence is denied, it is fair to argue that there must be some adequate sanction for the moral law in a life other than this, for here the sanctions are inadequate.

21 The body is the soul's partner in good and bad acts, and both must be rewarded together.

22 Virtue and vice are not merely spiritual qualities.

23 Nor is the soul alone subject to the moral law.

24 ARGUMENT FROM THE END OF MAN: The end of man is not oblivion or mere pleasure,

25 nor is it achieved in the separation of the soul from the
body. Hence there must be a reconstitution.

THE PLATONISM OF ATHENAGORAS

In the time of Athenagoras, Tertullian was to write that
Plato was the sauce merchant used by all the heretics,[19]
and Tatian was to produce a diatribe against the classics.
It is surprising then that Athenagoras himself should show
such sympathy for Platonic ways of thought, but, if his
earlier life had been that of an exponent of Plato's philosophy (as the preceding discussion has shown to be likely),
then one can understand this difference of attitude very
well. One cannot for all that claim that with Athenagoras
Christianity was a veneer upon a Platonic habit of thought
which survived unchanged from his days as a pagan
lecturer. His firm rejection of the transmigration of souls
is proof enough of that.

His technique in developing an argument is manifestly
Platonic: there is the analogy from agriculture and the
manual arts brought in to suggest lines of thought; the
derivation game is played in the manner of the *Cratylus*,
and in the account of the digestive process—which
Athenagoras finds himself involved in when facing difficulties alleged against the resurrection of the body—the
behaviour of stronger and weaker forces in attacking or
retiring before the attacker is very much like that of the
rival forms described in the *Phaedo*. Stock Platonic
themes, like the attack on the poets as teachers of immorality and the value of the argument from design, are used
where there is no possibility of conflict with Christian
thought. Formal citation of passages from Plato is not

often resorted to, and one can count them on the fingers
of two hands. The *Republic, Gorgias, Phaedo, Phaedrus,
Timaeus* (twice), *Politicus,* and *Second Epistle* make up the
total.[20] The very fact that the *Embassy* of Athenagoras
was to a philosopher king does not pass unnoticed, and it
is taken for granted that the Laws can be personified.

Athenagoras expressly states that Plato was no atheist,
but he does not want to call him a Christian before his
time, and there is no sign that the stories of Plato's having
studied the Old Testament during his visit to Egypt were
believed by Athenagoras, though they had been accepted
by Justin[21] a generation earlier, and in this Clement of
Alexandria followed Justin avidly. One expects therefore that there will be certain departures from Plato on the
general subjects of the knowledge of God's nature, the
ideas, creation, the human soul and its spiritual life, and
the final destiny of mankind. A few remarks on each of
these topics may bring out the extent to which Athenagoras has been adapting Plato to his own Christian needs.
One could speculate on the possible influence that this
adaptation by Athenagoras might have had, if his work had
been more widely known in antiquity, or one might
examine what in fact is the debt of Clement of Alexandria
to one who, on the evidence already submitted, might
possibly be regarded as his teacher, but neither of these
tasks falls within the scope of the present work.

God is accessible to *Nous* alone, says Athenagoras[22] in
a sentence that Plato might have written, but, when he
wants a word for God's inaccessibility, it is to St. Paul's
vocabulary that he turns and not to the language of the
Platonic way of negation. In listing the divine attributes,
he gives first the negative ones, then those which men
represent to themselves as their own perfections purified,

and finally settles on the unique creative activity of God which makes His transcendence more clear to mortals. In the *Embassy*[23] he has the analogy of action between God the craftsman and the Athenian potter, but he does not there develop this analogy. In the *Resurrection*[24] he is more explicit. In ch. 12 he makes what must be regarded as the first Christian use of the analogy of being in a philosophical argument. The cause 'that is comprehended within the nature and regarded only in the aspect of one that exists,' is perhaps a cumbersome way of saying that God and man share in the analogous predicate of being or existence, but it is too explicit to leave room for any doubt. The extent to which Platonic philosophers had succeeded by the end of the 2nd century in producing the idea of the analogy of being out of the hints that Plato gives may be disputed, but there can be no doubt that Athenagoras had it.

Goodness is an inseparable accident of God's nature for Athenagoras,[25] and herein he differs widely from Plato. There was always a problem for the Platonic scholar, whether to make the highest in the hierarchy of forms a soul or not, and those Platonists who held that the form of the Good *was* the highest soul, or God, by actual identification, found it hard to avoid saying that God must of necessity produce emanations of Himself, since the Good is communicative of itself by its very nature. Athenagoras by making God's goodness an inseparable property of His being, as natural to Him as a skin is to a body or their ruddy colour to flames of fire, seems to be seeking to avoid having to say that God must of necessity communicate His being by some kind of creation. He uses a strictly non-technical word ἀποχεόμενον for the over-spill of God's goodness upon the world, and the terms πρόοδος and ἐπιστροφή, which are the regular words used by Neo-Platonists for the outflow of being from the One and for its return thereto, are not found in his work.

Clement of Alexandria [26] will be found quite ready to take over the Platonic theory that the Ideas are somehow in God as in a place, but there is no trace of this in Athenagoras. The Stoics had taken up this particular feature of Plato's theology, and Seneca could write: [27]

> God hath the patterns and examples of all things in Himself. He hath conceived in His understanding the members and fashions of all that which should be made by Him. He is full of all those forms and figures which Plato calleth ideas, which are immortal, immutable, and indefatigable.

Athenagoras does indeed speak of God the Son as the thought and power (ἰδέα καὶ ἐνέργεια) of the Father and says that all things were made through Him and after His fashion, or agreeably to Him. In this he is following the Prologue of St. John more closely than anything that is specifically Platonic. From the philosophical point of view his language is studiously vague, and attempts to sharpen its definition by changing πρὸς αὐτοῦ into πρὸς αὐτόν in *Embassy* 10 are quite misguided.

Plato had distinguished [28] causes that work with intelligence to produce what is good from those which gave rise to random and disorderly effects, and he recognized the presence of a surd element in the world as at present constituted. Athenagoras is not anxious to accept the full opposition of Love and Strife as it had descended to the later Greek philosophers from Empedocles, and he draws less upon this idea than Plato himself did. The devil is God's adversary, according to Athenagoras, [29] and he is looked upon as having some powers in this sublunary world of matter. He has sinned by neglecting his charge, and his offence is distinguished from that of the lustful angels who according to the old Jewish tale begot the giants. The devil is not the counterpart to God's being, but to His goodness, which goodness has been declared to belong to, but not to be identified with, God's being. Thus Athenagoras finds a rather primitive way of avoiding the dualism which in his Gnostic surroundings must have been very catching. That he should avoid it says much for his integrity as a Christian thinker. The picture of Zeus making royal progress through the heavens in his winged chariot followed by the swarm of lesser gods is cited from the *Phaedrus* in *Embassy* 23, but Athenagoras appeals to it only to show that Plato had travelled some distance on the long road from belief in many gods to a pure monotheism. One never has the impression that the Christian author was willing to meet him halfway. What is perhaps surprising is the lack of all reference to the tenth book of the *Laws* where Plato set down his natural theology with all the completeness it was ever to have.

One notable difference between Athenagoras and his master is in the account of the human soul. Whereas Plato has accepted the threefold division of the soul, Athenagoras has abandoned it for a twofold division [30] and he is one of the first to introduce us to the term συναμφ-ότερον or *compositum*. Even among the Stoics man was held to be made up of body, spirit, and mind, and Jewish thought also had accepted this threefold division. The third member, mind, was to the Stoic a participation in the divinity, and Athenagoras, in order to avoid falling into this form of paganism, may have been content to accept as much of this account as he could, holding man to be body and spirit and making his mind to be independent of that of God and somehow to be identified with his spirit. The soul is still the body's rider as in Plato's *Phaedrus*, but it is now held that each member of the *compositum* has to make its own contribution to the common stock of existence. Partnership rather than opposition is the keynote of their relation, and the Platonic notion of the body as a prison house has been set aside.

There is an absence of sex-differentiation in human souls considered by themselves, both for Plato and for Athenagoras, and in the *Resurrection*, ch. 18, Athenagoras professes the belief that the soul is not 'engaged' when the body is caught up in sexual excesses, a view that might have come from the *Timaeus*. Plato's conclusion there suggested that no one is bad of his own will is not accepted by Athenagoras, who holds that the body at least is due for punishment for such excesses. He does not, however, go on to find the flaw in the argument and to declare the soul part-responsible for the excess by its omission to control its onset. The somewhat Pelagian position of Plato that knowledge is virtue, or is so near to it as to make no difference, is not taken by Athenagoras, who has no reference to the discussion on piety in the *Euthyphro*. One might have thought that it would have been easy to present to the emperors the idea of baptism as a purification after the manner of those καθαρμοί which figure in Pythagorean practice, but there were Gnostic excesses of all kinds in connexion with baptism and Athenagoras has kept silence about it in both his works.

Plato believed in a providence,[31] though he had no real expectancy of a divine revelation. To a Christian such as Athenagoras God's revelation was indeed a work of providence, and even more than that, being simply 'too good to be true,' or an excess of goodness beyond human ex-

pectation. Providence requires a judgment for the end of
the world, and Plato's Minos and Rhadamanthus, whatever value they may have had for himself, are now quite
transcended, for now they will themselves have to submit
to the judgment of Christ. When Plato said [32] that it was a
hard task to find the Maker of this universe and impossible
to declare Him to the rest of mankind, he seemed to a
Christian to hover on the verge of the idea of a revelation.
One had only to put his premiss into relation with the
other idea that God exercises a providential care over the
world, to produce if not a conclusion at least a suspicion
that there would be a revelation from God to lighten
man's task. Athenagoras is so sure of God's revelation
from his Christian faith, that he can afford to retain much
of the philosophy of his former master Plato, as leading
thereto.

THE TRINITARIAN DOCTRINE OF ATHENAGORAS

Plato was familiar with the first pair of friendly numbers
(i.e. 220 and 284) between which a κοινωνία of a peculiar
kind exists so that the factors of the one, when added up,
give the other number, and vice versa. This numerical
phenomenon led him to accept a kinship between forms
not quite after the same fashion but understandable by the
numerical analogy. That persons and divine persons, too,
should have such κοινωνία was more than Plato dreamt
of, but it is in these terms [33] that Athenagoras describes the
divine relations. Father and Son are one by the *kinship*
of the Spirit. Some interpreters of his work have made him
say that it is by kinship in one divine *nature* that the Three
are one, but that would be to make the Divine Persons no
better than the instances of a universal, like men sharing

in a common humanity. He can hardly have meant this. If he had said that the *Three* Persons were one by the unity of the divine nature, that would be unexceptionable, but to say that Father and Son as Persons are one by that nature is to make the divine relations of no account. A modern theologian might say that Father and Son are one in their common Spiration of the Holy Spirit, and that Son and Spirit are somehow one in their Proceeding from the Father. When *kinship* is being considered, it is inevitably to the relations that one must turn and not to the common nature of the godhead. That Athenagoras should make this kinship of Father and Son their oneness in the Holy Spirit is only a simplified way of saying that they combine to breathe forth the Spirit, and it may be that he would have claimed justification for his phrase in the doxology of the prayers of the Church.

In describing how the Son proceeds by generation from the Father, Athenagoras is obviously embarrassed and his language becomes involved. That he should call the Father λογικός, or 'possessed of a Word,' does not however mean that he thought of the Word prior to the temporal generation as a mere faculty of the Father's being. At such an early stage of theological speculation one must allow for a certain roughness and imprecision of language which later speculation will remove. The eternal existence of the Word is affirmed [34] most categorically, while at the same time it is allowed that the Word became possessed of a relationship of some kind to matter when creation had taken place. This relationship is not further defined as one of exemplary causality, but that idea cannot have been far from the thought of Athenagoras.

The Spirit is described as an outflow from God, coming forth and returning like a ray of light.[35] Elsewhere it is

said that God *is* light. The exact relationship of the Spirit
to the other Divine Persons is not touched upon in what
is meant to be a summary account of Christian belief for
a pagan audience, and one cannot press the statement
about the Spirit as being an admission of the dependence
and inferiority of that Divine Person. Justin had used the
same image to describe how the Son came forth from the
Father: Athenagoras has carried it over into another
relationship, but seems by his choice of a distinctive term
not hitherto used in this connexion to wish to mark a
certain difference between this outflow and one that leaves
the product inferior to the producer. Had Christianity
developed a metaphysic in terms of light rather than of
being, the language of Athenagoras would easily have
fallen into place.

The intellectual generation of the Son from the Father
seems to be expressed in a passing phrase at one point in
the *Embassy*, for the adjective νοούμενος is given to the
Son along with the other predicate of 'inseparable' and
in a completely parallel position with it. The extent to
which a technical vocabulary of such terms had been
developed by this time is always hard to judge because
we know so little of the details of the discussions which
must have taken place among Christians themselves about
the mysteries of the faith at this time. Almost all the surviving literature of the first Christian century is made up
of apologetic works addressed to pagans and occasional
letters which did not allow their writers much scope for
such discussion. One is therefore justified in making the
most of such technical terms as are let fall by such a
writer as Athenagoras, and it would be wrong to mini-
mize their importance. He only once uses the technical
term for the Incarnation (οἰκονομία), which we know to

have been established long before his day, and one can infer from this that solitary occurrences of other terms that seem to be technical are quite reasonably taken as implying their free use elsewhere by the writer.

One cannot make out much of the creed known to, or recited by, Athenagoras. It may be that he was familiar with a two-member creed[36] which was lacking in all mention of the Holy Spirit and the Church, but the evidence is not sufficient to establish such a conclusion.

ATHENAGORAS AND THE LITURGY

One does not expect direct quotation from the liturgical prayers of the Church in a work of apologetic addressed to pagans. It is none the less true that in *Embassy* 13 Athenagoras seems to be quoting from a public prayer in praise of the Creator—'who stretched out the heavens and reared them into a vault and established the earth as centre of things, who gathered the waters into seas and separated light from darkness, who bedecked the sky with stars and made the earth bud forth every green thing, who made the animals and fashioned man.' Similar prayers are to be found in Melito's *Homily on the Passion* and in the *Apostolic Constitutions*.[37] One may readily infer, from Athenagoras's mention in this context of the sacrifice of praise, when Christians raise holy hands to God, that his prayer would go on to speak of Christ who at the end of ages, in the night before He suffered, took bread and . . . ; exactly as so many anaphora prayers of antiquity declare to us.

Athenagoras certainly deserves the credit for introducing into the vocabulary of Christian theology the term 'un-

bloody sacrifice.' The adjective is not found in the Septua-
gint, the New Testament, the Apostolic Fathers, or in
the Apologists.[38] When he has quoted the prayer of praise
to the Creator here given and has reprobated the animal
sacrifices of the pagans, he then concludes that the only
reasonable worship is an unbloody sacrifice such as the
Christians offer to God. He speaks of this bloodless sacrifice
being 'brought forward,' and in the context it is hard to
avoid the idea that he looks upon the chief act of Christian
worship as a sacrifice, where the sword is a word and where
no blood is shed, but where something recognizable as a
sacrifice takes place. It would thus be hard to deny that
for him the Eucharist was a sacrifice. If he were speaking
of prayer merely, he would not use the term προσάγειν.

The kiss of peace at the Christian liturgy is mentioned
by Athenagoras,[39] and he is our sole witness for the law
that it was to be given once only by each person present.
Clement of Alexandria complains of overmuch kissing
in the Christian assembly, but apart from this one chance
reference by Athenagoras all knowledge of any legislation
on the subject before A.D. 300 would have perished. The
implication of the law is that the kiss of peace was still
given by men to women and by women to men without
separation of the sexes on either side of the church.

A minor liturgical reminiscence seems to have survived
at the end of *Embassy* 10, where a Trinitarian phrase
echoes the style of many later prayers to the Trinity
including our own Preface of the Trinity. The words:
We 'call God Father and Son and Holy Spirit, proclaiming their power in unity and in rank their diversity,' have
the articulation of later Trinitarian prayers with the balance
of contrasting clauses. That Christians of the period did
call upon the Trinity is shown by the hymn which runs:

'As we sing to Father Son and Holy Spirit, may all the powers join with us to say Amen. To the only giver of all good things be power and praise. Amen.'[40]

⟱ ⟱ ⟱

The text of the *Embassy* which has been used for the present translation is that of Geffcken published in *Zwei griechische Apologeten* (Leipzig—Berlin 1907), while for the *Resurrection* the text of Schwartz from *Texte und Untersuchungen* 4.2 (Leipzig 1891) has been followed. Where the translator has felt bound to depart from these two texts, mention of the fact is made in the notes.

The only previous translation of both works into English known to the writer is that of B. P. Pratten in *Ante-Nicene Christian Library* 2 (Edinburgh 1869) 371–456. A French version of the *Embassy* has recently been made by Canon G. Bardy in *Sources chrétiennes* 3 (Paris 1943). An Italian version by P. Ubaldi was published at Turin in 1913 and the same author produced an edition of the text in 1920, re-edited in 1933 and again in 1947 (with his pupil, M. Pellegrino, as vol. 15 of the series *Corona Patrum Salesiana, Serie Greca*).

The *Resurrection* was first printed by Petrus Nannius (Louvain—Paris 1541) and was twice reprinted before the complete edition of both works came from the press of Henricus Stephanus at Paris in 1557. Among later editions, that of Otto in the *Corpus Apologetarum* (Jenà 1857) should be mentioned. The edition of the *Embassy* by Goodspeed (Göttingen 1914) has also been found useful. I have not seen the German translation of both works by A. Eberhard in *Bibliothek der Kirchenväter* 23 (Kempten 1913). The *Studi sul antica Apologetica* (Rome 1947) of Pellegrino have been found useful and, though the analysis here given was made independently of his, the result will be found to correspond at most points.

The version of the *Embassy* by C. C. Richardson in the first volume of the *Library of Christian Classics* (*Early Christian Fathers* [London 1953] 290–340) appeared while this work was being prepared for the press. The present version was then compared closely with Richardson's, and one or two modifications were made. The writer cannot agree with Richardson that the work should be called a *Plea*, rather than an *Embassy*, for though the Greek title can be used in both senses, the words in *Embassy* 11, which imply an address to the emperor face to face, cannot be set aside as mere rhetoric, especially in view of the historical basis which is now quite generally allowed for the many pagan embassies to the emperors from Alexandria between A.D. 35 and 180. The summing up by H. A. Musurillo (*Acts of the Pagan Martyrs* [Oxford 1954] 275) should warn the reader that the opinion of Richardson (which is supported by P. Keseling in the article on Athenagoras in the *Reallexikon für Antike und Christentum* 1 [Stuttgart 1950] 881) has been antiquated by the more recent evidence.

EMBASSY FOR THE CHRISTIANS

To the Emperors Marcus Aurelius Antoninus and Lucius Aurelius Commodus, Armenian and Sarmatian Victors, and, what is more, Philosophers.

[EXORDIUM]

1. Your world empire, great sovereigns, uses one customary law here and another there,[1] nor is anyone ever restrained by legal process and fear of constraint from showing affection towards his ancestral uses however ridiculous they may be.[2] The man of Ilium calls Hector a god[3] and wittingly does homage to Helen[4] as his goddess of Necessity; the Lacedaemonian calls Agamemnon Zeus[5] and reverences Phylonoe,[6] daughter of Tyndareus, in the guise of Enodia[7]; the Athenian offers sacrifice to Erectheus[8] as to Poseidon, and both for Athene Agraulos and for Pandrosos[9] the Athenians celebrate initiation ceremonies and mysteries, Pandrosos and the other maidens being deemed to have fallen into sin when they opened the chest. In short, men keep what sacrifices they will and what mysteries, differing among themselves by country and by place.[10] In Egypt even cats and crocodiles, snakes, asps, serpents, and dogs are revered as gods.[11] All these you and your laws leave unmolested, deeming it wicked and impious not to venerate gods at all and a bounden duty for each to honour as gods those whom he would, that thus a fear of the divine power may keep men from wrong-doing.

29

Pray, do not be led astray by hearsay as happens to the man in the street: to us [12] hatred is shown [13] because of our name. Yet names are not deserving of hatred; it is wrong-doing that should be judged and chastised. Hence it is that the individual, marvelling at your meekness and gentleness and your peaceable, friendly ways with all men, lives in equality before the law; cities, according to their deserts, enjoy equality of prestige, and the whole world rejoices in a profound peace [14] through your enlightenment.

Now with us who are called Christians, so far are you from caring for people like us that you allow us to be harried, robbed, and pursued though we do no wrong and are—as this work will show in due course—of all men the most reverent and righteous in matters that concern God and your kingdom. Thus when the mob is at enmity with us for our name's sake alone, [15] we have made so bold as to declare to you our position. You will learn from our account that we suffer injustice in violation of all law and reason. We ask you to pay some heed even to us that there may be an end to our being slaughtered by lying informers. The punishment these persecutors inflict is not a fine levied on our goods nor a besmirching of our honour as citizens, nor is the harm done us some petty annoyance. These in fact we despise, even though some may think them matters of concern. We have learnt not to strike back when we are flogged nor to go to law with those who rob and despoil us. [16] When they abuse us and strike us on one cheek, we let them strike the other, too, and if they snatch our tunic from us, we give them our cloak besides. No, it is against the life of our bodies that they plot, when we have been drained of our wealth; they hurl upon us accusations of a host of crimes which it has really never even crossed our minds to perpetrate [17] but which are proper to idlers and men of that sort.

2. Now if a man has any charge great or small on which he can secure a conviction, we do not refuse to be punished, but think it right that we should undergo the bitterest and most merciless penalty. But if the accusation stops short at our name—and up to the present no Christian has been found guilty of the things which the general and uncontrolled report of men has fabricated about us— it befits you as great, beneficent, and wise rulers to devise for us some aid of the law against this calumny, that just as the whole world has enjoyed your beneficence, [18] both individually and city by city, we in our turn may pay thanks to you in our homage for being rid of false accusers. Nor is it in accord with your justice that others who have set their hands to evil should remain unpunished until they are proved guilty, whilst against us our name [19] should be a greater handicap than conviction in a court. Our judges do not seek to know if one of us has done evil, but heap abuse upon our name as though that were itself an injustice. But no name, by itself and for itself, is considered to be bad or good, but it acquires an appearance of good or evil from the good or evil deeds that accompany it. This you know very clearly from your education in philosophy and all manner of culture. Hence, too, those who are judged in your presence are of good heart even when they are being tried for their lives: they know that you will examine their lives and not give heed to mere empty names nor to lying accusations from the prosecution, and are ready to accept from you the pebble of condemnation as easily as that of acquittal.

We too, then, beg to enjoy this equity of yours towards all and not to be objects of hatred and castigation because we are called Christians—for what evil does our name produce by itself?—but to be judged for anything that anyone may lay to our account. Let us be discharged when we explain away the charges or let us be punished if found to be guilty; not guilty of our name merely—for no Christian is wicked unless he play false to his profession—but guilty of a crime. We observe that the disciples of philosophers are judged in this way. Before judgment none of them is considered by the judge to be good or bad just on account of his learning or skill: it is when found to be evil that he is punished. He draws down no extra accusation upon his philosophy, but rather, if he rebut the slanders, he is set free: it is the man who philosophizes contrary to the law of reason who is judged evil, but his learning itself is guiltless. Let us meet with the same equity.[20] When a man is on trial, let his life be examined, but let his name be beyond any charge. I have perforce, great Emperors, in beginning my apology for our profession, to ask you to be equitable listeners to us and not to be carried away at the outset and held in thrall by common and senseless rumour, but to direct your love of truth and sound knowledge upon the account of ourselves that follows. Thus you will not be victimized by ignorance, and we, once we are set free from the results of uncritical rumour among the multitude, shall have no more enemies to meet.[21]

[PLAN OF SPEECH]

3. Three charges are brought against us by rumour[22]: godlessness, Thyestean banquets, and intercourse such as Oedipus practised. Now if these charges are true, spare no class amongst us, but proceed against these crimes and

extirpate us, women and children too; if, that is, any
human being could be found thus to live in the manner of
beasts. And yet beasts actually refrain from those of their
own blood and have intercourse only when nature prompts
them to the begetting of offspring, not for mere wantonness: they know moreover who are their helpers.[23] If then
there be a man who is more savage than the beasts, what
punishment should he not undergo, to be worthily punished for such evils? But if these charges are fictions and
empty slanders—vice being the natural opposite of virtue
and by divine law a contest[24] being engaged between the
two—and if you bear witness that we do none of these
evil things by issuing your order forbidding anonymous
informers,[25] it remains for you to make an investigation
into our lives, our opinions, our zealous obedience towards you and your house and government, and in so
doing to show no more favour to us than to our accusers.[26]
Assuredly we shall overcome them; we are ready without
hesitation to give even our lives for the truth.

[REPLY TO FIRST CHARGE: ATHEISM]

4. I shall now answer the charges in succession. That
we are not atheists is so clear that it might seem ridiculous
to begin a refutation of those who make the charge. The
Athenians were right to charge Diagoras[27] with it, since
he not merely jeopardized the Orphic doctrine and made
public the mysteries of Eleusis and those of the Cabiri,
and cut down the wooden statue of Heracles to boil his
turnips, but also because he ventured to declare openly
that there was no god at all. Now when we make a distinction between matter and God and show that matter is one

being while God is quite other, completely separated from the former—for the divine is unbegotten and invisible, beheld only by mind and thought, while matter is subject to generation and corruption—surely it is unreasonable of them to charge us with atheism. If our opinions were like those of Diagoras, in spite of our having so many sure signs that encourage us to piety in the order, the complete harmony,[28] the extent, the colours and shapes and the planning of the universe, it would be reasonable to fasten on us the reputation of being atheists and make us liable to banishment. But when our doctrine introduces one God, creator of all this world, Himself unbegotten (for it is not Being that is subject to Becoming,[29] but not-Being), and says that all things are made by the Word that proceeds from Him,[30] we are wrongfully assailed on both sides by our calumniators and by our prosecutors.

5. Poets and philosophers were never deemed atheists for being curious about God. Euripides, perplexed about those that are foolishly named gods by common intelligence, says: 'Zeus, if there be a Zeus in heaven, ought not to make the same man wretched'[31]; but when he is considering what is intelligible by pure reason, he lays it down that there is a God:

> Dost see this aether stretching infinite,
> And girdling earth with close yet soft embrace?
> That reckon thou thy Zeus, that name thy God.[32]

He saw that no substance underlay those upon whom the name of God had chanced to be set as a predicate:

> Zeus, whate'er Zeus may be (for, save by hearsay, I know not)—

and that the names were not predicated of real subjects,

for where no substance is the ground of being, what else is there but a name? Realizing then that appearances give us sight of the invisible, he saw that there was a God from His works in air, sky, and earth.[33] The one whose works they are and whose Spirit governs all, Him he took to be God; and Sophocles[34] agreed with him, saying with reference to the nature of God who fills heaven and earth with His beauty:

> In very truth one God there is,
> One who has fashioned heaven and the broad earth—

thus teaching both that God must be one and where He must be.

6. Yes, and Philolaus[35] too, who says that everything is kept fast bound in ward by God, declares that He is one and that He is above matter. So it is with Lysis and Opsimus: the one defines God to be a number that cannot be uttered,[36] the other calls Him the excess of the greatest number above its next neighbour.[37] Now if ten is the greatest number according to the Pythagoreans, since it is four-square[38] and comprises all arithmetical and harmonic ratios, and since nine is the number next to this, then God is a unit; that is to say, God is one, for the greatest surpasses its next neighbour on the lower side by one.

I will run through what Plato and Aristotle have said about God, though not indeed with the intention of giving an exact account of the beliefs of these philosophers. I know that just as you surpass all in the wisdom and might of your rule, in the same measure you are superior to all in your accurate knowledge of all kinds of learning and can make your way along any path of culture more successfully than those who have chosen to specialize on that very subject. Since, however, it is impossible to show without

a setting-down of names that we are not the only ones to
confine God to a monad, I was minded to turn to the
Doxographers.[38a] Plato then says: 'It is difficult to discover the maker and sire of this universe, and when one
has found Him, one cannot speak of Him to the multitude.'[39] He considered that the unbegotten and unseen
God is one. If he is prepared to recognize others, such as
sun, moon, and stars, it is as begotten that he admits
them: 'Gods of gods whereof I am the maker, and of
works the Father that are indissoluble save with my con-
sent, even though whatsoever bond has been fastened may
be loosed.'[40] If now Plato is no atheist, recognizing one
unbegotten God as the maker of all things, neither are we
atheists, since we know and cherish[41] that being as God
by whose Word all things are made and by whose Spirit
all things are held in being.

Aristotle and his followers, producing as it were a
composite living being, declare that God consists of soul
and body, deeming His body to be the etherial region, the
planets and the sphere of the fixed stars, all in circular
motion, and His soul to be the reason that guides the
motion of the body—itself unmoved, while being cause
of motion to the other.[42] The Stoic school, even though
they amass a multitude of names for the divine being,
according as it has to be named to suit the changes of matter
through which they say that the 'Breath' of God passes,
do in reality reckon God to be one. For if God is that
artisan fire which, making its way towards the production
of the universe, embraces all the 'seminal reasons' after
the pattern of which each group of things comes to be in
its appointed order, and if the Spirit of God pervades the
whole universe, then God is one in their philosophy,
being named Zeus in the fiery element[43] of matter, Hera

in the element of air, and having other names for the other portions of matter in which He is contained.

7. Seeing therefore that practically all agree even against their will, when they come down to first principles, that the divine being is somehow one, and we on our part confirm that this being who has arrayed all this universe throughout is God, why is it that they can speak and write [44] as they will about the divinity, while a law is set against us [45] who are able to prove from evidence and arguments based on truth what we think and believe, namely that God is one? Poets and philosophers fell to this task as to others by guess-work: each was stirred by his own soul through some sympathy [46] with the 'Breath' from God to go upon the quest if haply he might find and understand the truth; they were able to find that only which came within the scope of their minds, but not to find the reality—not deigning to learn about God from God, but each from himself. Thus it is that each of them came to form differing beliefs about God and matter, about forms and the universe. We on our side have prophets[47] as witnesses of our ideas and beliefs, men who have spoken out under divine inspiration [48] about God and the things of God. You yourselves might perhaps admit, with your superiority to others in wisdom and reverence for the true divinity, how unreasonable it is to abandon faith in the Spirit of God who moves the lips of the prophets as if they were musical instruments, and to give ear to merely human beliefs.

8. That the maker of this universe from the beginning is really one God, there is the following argument to consider; you may then understand the reasoning upon which our faith rests. If there were from the beginning two gods [49] or more, either they were in one and the same

genus, or each of them was independent. Now they could not be in one and the same genus, for (a) if they were gods, they were not like each other, but being uncreated were unlike (created things are like their models and uncreated things unlike, having no relation to a model or to an origin); if, however, (b) these beings were complementary parts of a natural kind—like hand, eye, and foot in one body—making a complete whole out of themselves, then God would still be one. Thus, Socrates, since he was begotten mortal, can be divided up into parts, whereas God is unbegotten, impassible, and indivisible, and so is not composed of parts. If, on the other hand, (c) each one of them is independent, and the creator of the universe is above the created beings which He has made and adorned, where is the *other* god or the rest of them? For if the universe, being created spherical, is rounded off by the circle of the heavens and the maker of the universe is above His creation, checking it by His providence over all creation, where is there room for the second god or the others? It cannot be in the universe, for that is another's, nor are they outside the universe, for the god who made the universe is in charge of *that*. But if they are neither in the universe nor busy round about—for all that surrounds it is under the sway of the creator-god—where are they? Beyond God and the universe, in another universe and its sphere? But if the other god is in another universe and its sphere he is not in any way concerned with us, for he has no sway over this universe; nor is he almighty in power, for he is in a circumscribed place. If then he is not in another universe, for all space is filled up by this God, nor in charge of another universe, for everything is under the sway of this same God, then he does not exist, having no place in which to be.

What indeed is he to do, when there is another God whose universe this is, and he himself would be beyond the maker of this universe, yet having no universe to govern or in which to be? Can he then be entirely other, in such sort that he has some place in reality, when he comes to be over against the self-existent God? For again, God and what belongs to God are above him. And where will there be place for him when God fills up all that is beyond the universe? Well then, has he providential oversight over the universe? Not even that,[50] since he has not made the universe. Thus, if that other has no activity nor providence and there is no other place for him,[51] this one God, maker of the universe, is God alone and from the beginning.

9. If then we were content with these reasonings, one might consider our account of the matter to be true humanism. But the voice of the prophets guarantees our reasoning besides. (I expect that you who are so learned and so eager for truth are not without some introduction[52] to Moses, Isaias, Jeremias, and the rest of the prophets, who, when the Divine Spirit moved them, spoke out[53] what they were in travail with, their own reasoning falling into abeyance and the Spirit making use of them as a flautist might play upon his flute.) What then do these men say?[54] *The Lord is our God; no other shall be reckoned beside Him.* Again: *I, God, am the first and the last, and besides me there is no God.* Similarly: *Before me there was no other god formed, and after me there shall be none. I am God and there is no other apart from me.* And concerning His immensity: *Heaven is my throne and the earth my footstool. What is this house that you will build to me? And what the place of my rest?* I leave it to you, since you are possessed of the books themselves, to examine more closely the prophecies of

these men, in order that you may prepare with fitting reflexion to remove this obloquy from us.

10. I have given sufficient proof that we are not atheists, but hold God to be one, unbegotten, eternal, invisible, suffering nothing, comprehended by none, circumscribed by none,[55] apprehended by mind and reasoning alone, girt about with light and beauty and spirit and power indescribable, creator of all things by His Word, their embellisher and master. We do indeed think also that God has a Son[56]—and please let no one laugh at the idea of God having a Son! This is not a case of the myths of the poets who make the gods out to be no better than men; we have no such ideas about God the Father or the Son. The Son of God is Word of the Father in thought and power.[57] All things were made through Him and after His fashion.[58] The Father and Son are one. The Son being in the Father and the Father in the Son by the powerful union of the Spirit,[59] the Son of God is mind and Word of the Father. Now if, in your exceeding great sagacity, you wish to investigate what is meant by the Son, I will tell you in brief: He is the First-begotten[60] of the Father. He did not indeed come to be,[61] for God was from the beginning, being eternal mind, and had His Word within Himself, being from eternity possessed of a Word; but He proceeded to become thought and power over the elements of undifferentiated nature when all the material elements were like a substrate in quiescence and the heavier elements lay mixed with the lighter.

The Spirit of prophecy agrees with this account, saying: *The Lord made me the beginning of His ways for His works.*[62] Then again this same Holy Spirit, that works in those who utter prophecy, we call an outflow[63] from God, flowing out and returning like a ray of the sun. Who then would not be amazed hearing those called atheists who call God Father and Son and Holy Spirit, proclaiming their power in unity and in rank their diversity? Nor does our theology stop there, but we assert a multitude of angels and ministers [64] whom God, maker and artificer of the universe, set in their places by means of His Word and appointed severally to be in charge of the elements and the heavens and the universe and all it contains and its good order.

11. Do not be surprised that I am reproducing exactly the account customary amongst us. To prevent your being carried away by the unreasonable opinion of the multitude and to give you opportunity to know the truth, I give this exact report. By the dogmas to which we give assent, not man-made but divine and taught by God, we are able to persuade you that you have not to regard us as you would atheists. What are those sayings on which we are brought up? I shall tell you: *Love your enemies*; *bless them that curse you*; *pray for them that persecute you, that you may be the children of your Father who is in heaven, who maketh His sun to rise upon the good and the bad, and raineth upon the just and the unjust.* [65]

Now that I am come to a part of the message of God that has been made audible with much thunder, [66] allow me to fall back [67] upon my right to free speech, while I make my apologia before emperors who are also philosophers. Which of those who reduce syllogisms [68] or explain equivocal terms or trace out etymologies or tell us [69] of synonyms or homonyms, of categories and axioms, of subject and predicate, will undertake to render happy their associates through these and suchlike lessons, being so purified in soul as to love enemies [70] rather than to hate them and to bless those who are forward with their revilings instead of, as would be most reasonable, answering them back, and to pray for those who plot against their lives? On the contrary, such men are ever busy wickedly paying back things spoken ill of themselves[71]; and, being eager to work some mischief, they make their trade an artifice of words and not a manifestation of their deeds. But amongst us you might find simple folk,[72] artisans and old women, who, if they are unable to furnish in words the assistance[73] they derive from our doctrine, yet show in their deeds the advantage to others that accrues from their resolution. They do not rehearse words but show forth good deeds; struck, they do not strike back, plundered, they do not prosecute; to them that ask they give, and they love their neighbours as themselves.[74]

12. Surely then, if we did not think that God was in charge of human affairs, we would not thus cleanse ourselves. Such an idea cannot be maintained; but since we are convinced that we shall render an account of all our life here to God who made the universe and ourselves, we choose a modest, humane, and humble life, not deeming it so great an evil in this world if some rob us[75] of our life, as the good will be[76] which we shall get back from our great Judge in the shape of a gentle, humane, and equitable way of life on the other side. Plato said that Minos and Rhadamanthus will judge and punish the wicked,[77] but we deny that any, be he a Minos or a Rhadamanthus or the father of them both, will escape the judgment of God.

And yet those who think that this is the life to live— *Let us eat and drink, for tomorrow we die*[78]—and who consider death a deep sleep and a forgetting—'Sleep and Death are twin brothers'[79]—get the credit of being religious men: we, on the other hand, consider life in this world as brief and of little worth. We are guided by the Spirit[80] alone to know the true God and His Word, to know what is the unity of the Son with the Father, what the sharing[81] of the Father with the Son, and what the Spirit, to know what is the unity and division of these three great ones thus united—Spirit, Son, and Father. We know that the life that is in store is far better than can be described in words, if we depart pure from all stain. We are so far lovers of our fellows as not only to love our friends. *For, Scripture tells us, if you love them that love you and lend to them that lend to you, what reward shall you have?*[82] Are we, men like this, living such lives in order that we may escape condemnation, are we to be denied credence as men of religion?

These thoughts are but few out of many and trivial rather than lofty, but we do not wish to trouble you with more. Those who taste honey and whey[83] can tell if the whole be good by tasting even a small portion.

[First Objection to Reply]

13. The majority of those who accuse us of atheism have not even dreamt of the true idea of God and are bereft of understanding and insight[84] into true science and theology.[85] Consequently, judging piety by the practice of sacrificing,[86] they accuse us of not reverencing the gods of the city in each place. I beseech Your Majesties to hear my reply to both charges.

First, about our not sacrificing. The creator and Father of this universe needs no blood nor fat of sacrifice nor fragrance of flowers and incense, for He is Himself perfect fragrance,[87] needing nothing to make good defects nor any addition; but the best sacrifice to Him is for us to recognize who stretched out the heavens and reared them into a vault and established the earth as centre of things, who gathered the waters into seas and separated light from darkness, who bedecked the sky with stars and made the earth bud forth every green thing, who made the animals and fashioned man.[88] Whensoever we raise holy hands to God, whom we hold to be the creator, upholding all and overseeing all things[89] with wisdom and craft such as He employs in their guidance, what further need have we of hecatombs?

> The gods indeed by sacrifice and reverent prayer, by libation and burnt offering, do men overpersuade, making supplication whensoever anyone may transgress and commit sin.[90]

What need have I, pray, of whole burnt offerings, which God needs not? Though we do need to offer sacrifice, bringing forward a bloodless sacrifice, our reasonable service.[91]

14. The other charge, about our not approaching and reverencing the same gods as the cities, is very foolish. Our accusers charge us with atheism for not recognizing[92] the same gods as they, but they are in disagreement among themselves about gods: the Athenians have set up Celeus and Metaneira[93] as gods, the Spartans Menelaus,[94] to whom they offer sacrifice and hold festival. At Ilium where they will not even hear the name of the latter, they set up Hector.[95] The Ceans reverence Aristaeus,[96] who is to them both Zeus and Apollo; the Thasians, Theagenes,[97] who actually committed murder at the Olympic games; the Samians, Lysander[98] for all his murders and misdeeds; the Cilicians, Medea or Niobe;[99] the Sicels, Philip son of Butacides;[100] the people of Amathus, Onesilaus;[101] those of Carthage, Hamilcar.[102] Night would be on me before I

completed the catalogue. When there is all this disagreement about their gods, why do they accuse us for not
conforming? The conduct of the Egyptians [103] might even
seem to be ridiculous. On their holy days they beat their
breasts in the temples as if these beings were dead, and yet
they sacrifice to them as to gods. [104] And no wonder—
they actually regard animals as gods: they crop their hair
when the animals die, and bury them in temples and hold
public lamentations. If we are atheists for not joining in
with them in this worship, all cities and all peoples are
atheists, for not all admit the same beings as gods.

15. But suppose they all do admit the same. What then?
Since the multitude, not being able to distinguish what a
gulf there is between God and matter, approach with
reverence material idols, are we on their account to come
forward and worship their statues [105] when we know and
distinguish created from uncreated, being from not-being,
intellect from sense, and give each its proper name? If
God and matter are the same, two names for the one thing,
then we are atheists for not reverencing as gods stones and
wood, gold and silver. But if they are utterly different,
as far apart as the craftsman from the materials of his trade,
why are we being accused? As with the potter and his
clay, [106] the clay is material and the potter is the craftsman; so God is the craftsman and matter serves Him for
His craft. The clay cannot become vessels without craft,
and matter that is potentially all things did not receive its
differentiation and shape and order without God the
maker. [107] We do not regard the vessel as more worthy
of honour than its maker, nor the cups—even the gold
cups—as more honourable than the smith. If there be any
skill about their craftsmanship, we praise the craftsman,
and he receives the praise for them. Even so, with God

and matter, it is not matter that has the just praise and honour for the arrangement of beautiful things, but its maker, God. Therefore, if we consider the forms of matter to be gods,[108] we shall be deemed blind to the true God for equating fragile and mortal things[109] with the eternal.

16. The world is fair indeed, and excels in size and array[110] all that exists in the ecliptic and all that is about the Pole, and it excels too in the beauty of its spherical form; yet not this but its maker is to be adored. When provincials come to you, they do not turn aside from doing obeisance as is fitting to you their lords and masters— for it is from you that they would gain the boons they seek —nor do they run to admire the majesty of your dwelling; but, while they casually admire your royal home for its beautiful construction, when they arrive there, it is to you, their all-in-all,[111] they give their homage. Now you indeed as great kings have your dwellings fashioned in kingly style,[112] but the world did not come to be for any need on the part of God.[113] God is all-in-all to Himself, light inaccessible,[114] a universe of perfection, spirit, power, and reason. If then the world is a tuneful instrument[115] struck rhythmically, I reverence the one who put it in tune and plucked the strings and sang the harmonious accompaniment, but not the instrument itself. The stewards of the games do not pass over the lyre-players in the contest and go and crown their lyres. If, as Plato says, this world is God's craft,[116] then, marvelling at its beauty, I go to worship the craftsman. If the world is body and soul, as the Peripatetics say,[117] we do not give up our adoration of God who is the cause of bodily motion, and descend to weak and beggarly elements,[118] adoring passive matter along with impassible air as they do. If anyone sees powers[119] of God in the parts of the universe,

we do not go and adore the powers but their maker and master.

I do not ask of matter what it has not got, nor do I leave God to adore the elements which can do no more than what they have been told to do. If they are fair to look upon because of the maker's craft, they are yet transient by the very nature of matter. Plato too supports this argument: 'The being,' he says, 'which we have called heaven and universe has been endowed with many graces by the Father, but apart from these it partakes of bodily substance and therefore it cannot be free from change.' [120] If, then, while marvelling at the heavens and the elements for their craft, I do not adore them as gods, knowing their transient nature, how can I call those things gods which I know to have had men for their makers?

17. Let us now make a brief examination of these. One who is on his defence must be very exact even about the names of these gods, for they are novelties, and about their statues, [121] for they came into being, as one might say, only the other day. You yourselves know this more exactly than I, since you are well-versed in antiquity beyond ordinary men and in all its departments.

Now then, I claim that Orpheus, Homer, and Hesiod were the ones who gave names and pedigrees to the beings they called gods. Herodotus is my witness: 'I think that Homer and Hesiod preceded me by four hundred years, not more. They established the Greek theogony and gave the gods names, appointing their rank and functions and describing their appearance.' [122] The statues, while yet there was no art of modelling or painting or sculpturing, were not even dreamt of. [123] Then came the time of Saurios of Samos [124] and Crato of Sicyon and Cleanthes of Corinth [125] and the Corinthian maid. [126] The art of tracing out shadows was discovered by Saurios, who traced the outline of a horse as it stood in the sunlight, and the art of painting by Crato, who painted the outline of a man and a woman on a whitened tablet. The art of relief-modelling was discovered by the maid, for being enamoured of a youth, she drew the outline of his form on the wall as he slept, and then her father, a potter, delighted with the marvellous likeness, cut out a mould along this outline and filled it with clay. This mould of his is still preserved at Corinth. After these, Daedalus,[127] Theodorus, and Smilis[128] discovered the additional arts of statuary and modelling. The time interval, then, since statues and statue-making began is so short that I am able to mention the name of the craftsman of each god.

The statue of Artemis at Ephesus and of Athena—or rather of Athela, for the more initiate call her Athela,[129] as this was the ancient name for what came from the olive—... and Endoeus, a pupil of Daedalus,[130] produced the Seated Goddess. The Pythian Apollo[131] is the work of Theodorus[132] and Telecles, the Delian Apollo and Artemis are due to the skill of Tectaeus and Angelion.[133] The hands of Smilis produced the Hera of Samos and that of Argos, and Phidias produced the other idols. The Aphrodite of Cnidos is another work of Praxiteles's craft;[134] the Asclepius at Epidaurus is the work of Phidias.[135] To put it briefly, no single one of them has escaped being made by the hands of man. If then they are gods,[136] why did they not exist from the beginning? Why are they younger than their makers? Why did they require men of skill for their coming into existence? Earth, stone, wood, and a misapplied skill, that is what they are.

[Second Objection Countered]

18. Now some say that these are but images,[137] and that the gods are those after whose likeness the statues are made, and that, as for the processions that are made to these statues and the sacrifices offered to them and made for them, there is no other way in which one can approach the gods:

> For the gods are slow to show themselves clear to the beholder.[138]

They bring in proof of this the operations performed by certain statues; so let us examine the power which attaches to their names.

I beseech you, great Caesars, before my examination of this matter, to excuse me if I give you true reasonings. It is not my task to bring charges against idols, but while rebutting slanders I am going to give you our reasons for the choice we make.[139] May you succeed in searching out for yourselves [140] this heavenly kingdom also. Just as all is subject to you two, father and son, who have received the kingdom from God [141] (for the king's soul is in the hand of God, as the Spirit of prophecy [142] declares), even so to the one God and to His Word, Son by intellectual generation [143] and inseparable, all has been made subject.[144] Consider this, then, I beg you, before all the rest. The gods, they tell us, were not in existence from the beginning, but came into existence,[145] each of them, in like manner to ourselves. This is agreed to by all of them. Homer speaks of

> Oceanus, father of the gods, and mother Tethys;[146]

and Orpheus,[147] who was actually the first to discover their names and give an account of their pedigrees and

their several actions, and who is generally regarded as a
more accurate chronicler of the gods—for Homer usually
follows him, above all in theological matters—himself
declares their first origin to be from water:

Oceanus, who has been stablished origin of all.

According to him water was the origin of all things, and
from water slime was made; from these two an animal
was born, a dragon with a lion's head added ⟨and also a
bull's⟩ and between them the face of a god, and its name
was Heracles or Chronos. This Heracles produced a monstrous egg which, being filled by the power of its producer,
was by friction broken into two. The top half of it was
fashioned into Heaven and the lower part became Earth,
while from inside there came forth a two-bodied [148] hermaphrodite god. Heaven impregnated Earth and begot
daughters—Clotho, Lachesis, Atropos; and sons—Cottos
of the hundred hands, Gyges, Briareus, and the Cyclopes
—Brontes, Steropes, and Arges. These he bound and put
in Tartarus, having discovered that he was to lose his
kingdom at the hands of his children. Then Earth, being
angry, brought forth the Titans: [149]

> Lady Earth brought forth sons to Ouranos whom they call
>   by the name of Titans
> For the reason that they vengeance took upon mighty Ouranos
>   starry-crowned.[150]

19. This is the beginning of the gods' pedigree, in their
version of it, and of the universe. Consider it thus: [151]
How can each of these divinized beings be considered to
exist, as it did not exist in the beginning? For if they came
to be from nothing, as their own theologians relate, they
have no real being, for either a thing is unbegotten and

so immortal, or begotten and so corruptible. Now here
I am reasoning in no other wise than the philosophers:
'What is it that is always real and has no becoming, or
what is it that is always becoming but is never real?'
Plato, arguing about intelligence and sense, tells us that
enduring reality, the intelligible, is without beginning, but
that which has no reality, the sensible, comes to be and
has a beginning and an end.[152] By this argument too the
Stoics[153] say that everything will be burnt up[154] and come
to be again, when the universe starts on its new course.
They have two principles, one active and dominant, like
purposive intelligence, the other, passive and subordinate,
like matter: now, if it is impossible for the universe to
remain in the same state once it has come to be, even
though it is an object of providence, how can these gods
remain in their same condition, when they are not abiding
realities but things of time?[155] How are the gods better
off than matter, if they are made out of water? Why, even
on their view[156] it is not true that *all* things are made of
water. How in the first place could all things come to be
from simple elements of one species? Matter needs a craftsman and a craftsman matter. And how could their
figures[157] be made without matter or a craftsman?
Furthermore, it is not reasonable to postulate that matter
is more ancient than god,[158] for the efficient cause must
needs exist before the effects.

20. If now the incredible element in their theology
was confined to the declaration that the gods were creatures, and creatures made from water, it might be enough
for me to have shown that nothing coming to be is free
from corruption, and I might pass on to the remaining
accusations. But, to begin with, they have given us descrip-
tions of the bodies of these gods: Heracles is a coiled dragon

god; others are called the hundred-handed; and that daughter of Zeus, the one he had by his mother Rhea,[159] or by Demeter her daughter, has two eyes in the natural position and two more in her forehead, and at the back of her neck an animal's face, and horns too; and therefore Rhea, frightened by her monstrous birth,[160] fled away and did not give her suck, whence she was to the initiate Athela,[161] though called Persephone or Kore in common speech, not being the same as the Athena who is named from her character as maiden.[162]

Then, too, they have given an accurate description, as they think, of the doings of these gods, how Kronos gelded his father[163] and flung him from his chariot, and how he became a child-murderer, gulping down his male children. Zeus again bound his father and sent him to Tartarus, just as Ouranos had done with *his* sons, and warred with the Titans for the mastery; he pursued his mother Rhea when she refused marriage with him, turning into a serpent when she did so, and in that form binding her in the knot called after Heracles[164] and thus having intercourse with her—a fact which is symbolized in the staff of Hermes. Again, he violated his daughter Persephone, having intercourse with her, too, in a serpent's form, and so begetting Dionysus upon her.

All this had to be said. What is there of nobility or value in such tales to persuade us that Kronos, Zeus, Kore, and the rest are gods? Is it their bodily transformations? But who among mortals of sober judgment,[165] even when fallen into a trance, would accept that a viper was begotten by a god? Thus Orpheus:

Phanes gave birth to another dread child
From his sacred womb, the Viper dreadful to behold;

Locks of hair grew from its head and the face was fair to look
upon,
But all the rest below the neck was fearsome dragon.[166]

Who could believe that Phanes himself, being the first-
begotten of the gods—for he is the one that came out of the
egg—could have the form of a dragon, or be swallowed
by Zeus to make Zeus become incommensurable? If the
gods are in no way different from the vilest beasts, they
are not gods at all; for clearly it must be that the divinity
is separate from earthly things and from those derived
from matter. Why on earth do we approach them with
homage, when they are whelped like any cur and are
themselves ill-favoured and bestial in form?

21. If they merely said that they were embodied beings
with blood and seed and the emotions of anger and lust,
even then one would be bound to consider such an
account ridiculous,[167] for there can be neither anger nor
lust nor yearning nor life-giving seed in a god. Well then,
suppose them to be embodied, but masters of anger and
lust,[168] so that Athena may not be found:

> Wrathful with father Zeus,
> When fierce anger took hold of her;

and that Hera may not become a spectacle:

> Hera, whose breast could not contain her rage,
> But needs must she cry out.

Let them be masters of grief like this:

> Alack, a man beloved I discern
> Pursued around the wall; my heart is sad.

For my part I count mere men as fools and dull-witted
if they let anger and grief master them. But when the
father of gods and men bewails his son thus:

Woe is me, for Sarpedon my best-loved is fated to be quelled
By Patroclus, son of Menoetius,

and he cannot for all his grief snatch him from danger:

Sarpedon is son of Zeus,
But Zeus saves not his own son,

who would not blame as witless those who at such a price
are lovers of the gods—or rather atheists? Let their gods
be embodied, but do not let Aphrodite be wounded in her
body by Diomede:

Tydeus' son, the lordly Diomede hath run me through;

nor in her soul by Ares:

Aphrodite, daughter of Zeus, ever dishonours me[169]
For my lameness, and sets her heart upon Ares
The destroyer. . . .

[Ares,] the mighty in war, the ally of Zeus against the
Titans:

He rent the fair flesh,

he is presented as weaker than Diomede:

He raged as would Ares who brandisheth his spear.

Hush, Homer. A god is not mad with rage. Yet you tell
me of a god who is a murderer and the bane of men:

Ares, Ares, bane of men and murderer,

and you recount his adultery and bondage:

So these two went to the couch and lay down to sleep,
And about them the cunning toils of skilled Hephaestus
Clung fast, so that they could not move their limbs.

Do not the poets throw out a great spate of blasphemous

nonsense about the gods? Ouranos is gelded; Kronos is bound and sent to Tartarus; the Titans rise in revolt; Styx is slain in battle [170]—so they *do* admit that the gods are mortal. They fall in love with each other and with human beings:

> Aeneas the fair Aphrodite bore to Anchises,[171]
> Goddess wedded with a mortal, in the glens of Mount Ida.

No, they have no lust and no pain; for either they *are* gods, and passion does not take hold of them, or else. . . . Why, even if a god by divine dispensation [172] does take flesh upon himself, is he then at once passion's slave?

> Never once as thus did love of goddess or woman
> So quell the heart within my breast by its onset,
> Not when I loved the wife of Ixion,
> Nor when I loved Danae of the fair ankles, daughter of
>   Acrisius,
> Nor the far-famed daughter of Phoenix, nor even Semele,
> Nor Alcmene in Thebes, nor Demeter the fair-tressed queen,
> Nor glorious Leto, nor thyself.

Zeus is a creature, a corruptible being, with nothing of the god about him. The gods even act as servants to men:

> Halls of Admetus, in which I steeled myself
> To praise the helot's table, god though I was;

and as herdsmen:

> Coming to this land I herded for a stranger,
> And saved this house.

Admetus, then, is better than the god. O wise prophet, foreseeing what will befall others, didst thou then not foresee the murder of thy darling,[173] but didst slay with thy own hand thy friend?

I did indeed expect Apollo's divine mouth to be free
From lies, running over with prophetic craft,

says Aeschylus as he damns Apollo for a false prophet:

The very one who chants, he that was present at the feast,
He that told us this, he it is that slew my son.

22. Perhaps this is just poetic vagary, and there is some
scientific account of the gods in terms like this, spoken
by Empedocles:

Zeus is brightness and Hera source of life,[174]
And Aidoneus, and Nestis, who with her tears bedews the
mortal founts.

Well, if Zeus is fire, Hera earth,[175] Aidoneus air, and Nestis
water, these are elements—fire, water, air—and none of
them is a god, neither Zeus nor Hera nor Aidoneus. For
when matter was separated out by divine action, these had
their foundation and beginning—

Fire and water and earth and the kindly steep of air
And love amongst them all.

If they cannot without the action of love be kept from the
confusion which strife would cause, how can one call such
things gods? Love is Empedocles's governing principle,
the compounds are subordinate, and the governing principle is their lord. If therefore we suppose the 'power' of
governor and governed to be one and the same, quite
unawares we make corruptible, unstable, and changing
matter equal in rank with God the eternal, the unbegotten,
and the immutable.

For the Stoics Zeus is the fiery substance, Hera the air[176]
(by repeating the name several times over out loud, one
equates them), and Poseidon the 'potion.'[177] Each philoso-

pher has made up his own scientific account. Some call Zeus the double-natured air,[178] the hermaphrodite; others, the season that brings fine weather, and for this reason, they say, he alone escaped from Kronos. Against the Stoics one can urge that if you reckon the supreme god to be immortal and unbegotten, and that all that the process of change [179] contains is composite by nature, and if you say that the Spirit of God,[180] pervading matter, receives now this name, now that, according to the transformations of matter, then the varying shapes of matter will be the god's body; and when the elements waste away in the cosmic conflagration, their names will perish with their shapes, and the Spirit of God alone remain. Who could then believe those to be gods [181] whose bodies waste away in the passage of matter?

There is a reply to those who say that Kronos is time and that Rhea is earth, she conceiving by him and bearing a child, so as to be called the mother of all, and he begetting and swallowing up his child. They say that the castration of his vital parts signifies the congress of male and female, detaching and driving seed into the womb and bringing to birth a male having desire—that is, Aphrodite—in himself; and that the madness of Kronos is the change of season that withers all things living and the lifeless too; [182] and Tartarus and the bondage represent the time that changes with the seasons and vanishes out of sight. To all these we say: If Kronos is time, he moves on; if he is the season, he changes; if he is darkness or moisture or ice,[183] none of these abides. But the divine nature is immortal, immovable, and unchangeable. So neither Kronos nor his earthly symbol is a god.

As for Zeus, if he is air begotten by Kronos, Zeus being the male element and Hera the female—and thus she is his sister-wife—then he changes; and if he is season, he alters. But the divine nature is free from change and does not decay.

Why should I weary you by prolonging my discourse? You know better than I what each of the physical philosophers says, and what the writers have thought about the nature of the gods, about Athena, for instance, whom they call a prudence [184] that runs through all things, or what they say about Isis, whom they call birth of the aeon, out of which all are sprung and by virtue of which all exist, or about Osiris, [185] whose limbs Isis sought for and preserved in a grave after he had been slain by Typhon his monstrous [186] brother, which grave is still called Osiriaca. Twisting hither and thither among all manner of material things, they miss the god who is to be contemplated by reason; they deify the elements and portions of them, giving them now one name and now another. The sowing of corn is Osiris; hence they say that in the Mysteries on the finding of his limbs, or of the harvest-corn, it was said to Isis: 'We have found, we rejoice together.' Dionysus [187] is the grape, Semele is the vine-stock, and the thunderbolt is the fierce heat of the sun.

After all, they are doing anything but theology, those who divinize the myths. They little realize that they are strengthening the argument against the gods by all their apologies for them. What have Europa [188] and the bull or Leda [189] and the swan to do with earth and air? Is Zeus's shameful consorting with them to be a matter of earth and air? [190] They fail to see the greatness of God and cannot master it with their reason, for they have no insight [191] into the heavenly places. They waste their strength upon material objects and fall to making gods of the changeable elements. It is just as if a passenger reckoned a ship [192] in which he was sailing to be itself in the helmsman's place; it would still be no more than a ship, even if it was decked out in every way, as long as there was no helmsman. Just so, there is no point in having the elements of nature arrayed apart from the providence of God. The ship will not sail by itself, nor will the element be set in motion without the Demiurge.

23. Your surpassing wisdoms might ask me: How do some of the idols show activity, if those are not gods to whom we set up statues?

It is indeed not likely that lifeless and motionless statues will be able to move without someone to set them in motion. We do not of course deny that there are in certain places, cities, and countries some movements brought about by invocation of statues.[193] Still, we do not deem those to be gods who produce help for some and pain for others by their appropriate motions. We have in fact made a careful enquiry into the reasons why you think idols have certain powers, and into the names of those who man the idols and work through them. I must now call as witnesses even philosophers in my demonstration about the identity of the idol-operators, that they are not gods.

Thales,[194] as those tell us who knew his works well, was the first to make the division between god, spirits, and heroes.[195] He considers God to be the mind of the universe, spirits to be ensouled substances, and heroes the separated souls of men, the good heroes being good souls and the bad heroes bad souls. Plato, though abstaining from judgment about the rest of Thales's system, takes over this division between the uncreated god, those produced by the uncreated for the good order of the heavens—planets and fixed stars—and the spirits. About these spirits he excuses himself from speaking, drawing

5

attention to those who had spoken about them already:
'Concerning the other spiritual beings, to know and to
declare their generation is a task too high for ourselves;
we must trust those who have told it formerly; being, as
they said, offspring of the gods, they must beyond doubt
have had clear knowledge of their ancestors. We cannot
then refuse credence to the children of the gods, even
though they speak without probable or cogent proofs;
when they profess to report family matters, we must
follow the custom and accept what they say. Let us too,
then, hold and declare the account of the origin of these
gods which these tell us. As children of Earth and Ouranos
were born Oceanus and Tethys, and of these Phorcys, [196]
Kronos, Rhea and all their company; and of Kronos and
Rhea, Zeus and Hera and all their brothers and sisters
whose names we know, and of these yet other offspring.'

Did Plato, then, who came to understand that the eternal
mind, [197] even though apprehended by reason, was God,
and to detail its predicates—the true reality, the self-
begotten, the good proceeding from it which is truth—
did he consider it a task beyond his strength to attain to
the truth? When he had learned about the 'first power'
and how 'everything is dependent on the king of all
being for his sake and he the cause of all,' [198] and about
the 'second and third' ('the second principle is concerned
with the second objects and the third principle with the
thirds') [199] and about what are said to be the products of
those visible beings, heaven and earth, did he think it
beyond him to find out the truth? Surely one cannot say
that. But since he deemed it impossible for gods to beget
and be pregnant (for an end must come for all that comes
to be) and that it was still more impossible to persuade the
multitude who accept mythology without scrutiny, there-

fore he said [200] that it was beyond his power to know and
declare the birth of those other spirits, not being able to
discover or to say that gods are subject to birth at all.

His saying, then, that 'Zeus, the great leader in heaven,
driving his winged chariot, goeth first about to put all in
order and take care of all, and after him comes an army of
gods and spirits,' is not directed towards the Zeus that is
son of Kronos, for in this saying the name stands for the
maker of all things. Plato himself actually says this, being
unable to address him by any other designation. He uses
the popular name, not as proper to that god, but for sake
of clarity. Because it was not possible to present God to
the multitude, he did what he could, adding the epithet
'great' to mark off the heavenly [201] from the earthbound
Zeus, the uncreated from the created, who is younger than
heaven and earth, and younger than the Cretans who
carried him away to prevent his being slain by his father.

24. But why should I, when I have so much to say [202]
and you have examined the question already, recall
poets to your minds and examine other opinions? Is it
just for us to suffer banishment as aliens for drawing
distinctions between God and matter and their respective
substances, if in fact poets and philosophers had not already
on the one hand acknowledged the unity of God and then
gone on, some of them to think of the gods as spirits,
others as material and others as human creatures? For
we speak of His Word as God too and Son and of Holy
Spirit likewise, united into one by power and divided
in order thus, the Father, the Son, the Spirit, the Son being
mind, word, or wisdom of the Father and the Spirit an
effulgence as light from fire. Then we apprehend that
certain distinct powers exist that are in relation with
matter and use it, but that one of these is God's opposite.

Not that we consider there is a counterpart to God in the same way as with Empedocles strife is love's counterpart, or night is day's counterpart among sense objects, for if anything did stand counter to God, it would cease from existence, having the ground of its being dissolved by the power and might of God. No, we think rather that there is a counterpart to God's goodness. This goodness is annexed[203] to Him and coexistent with Him as surface is with body. It is nothing without Him, and, not being a part of Him, but, as it were, a necessary consequence of His being, so united and so closely allied to Him as the colour blue is to the sky or to fire its golden yellow. The counterpart is the 'spirit'[204] that is concerned with material things,[205] created by God just as other angels are created by Him, and entrusted by Him with the regulation of matter and its patterns. The calling into being of these angels was God's act in view of the providence they should have over what had been put in order by Him: thus while God had the general and creative providence over all,[206] these angels set over each part were to have providence over that part. And just as with men who have power to choose good or evil—for you would not honour the virtuous and punish evildoers if vice and virtue were not within their free choice—some are found zealous for what they are entrusted with by you, and others remiss, so it is with these angels too: some remained at the task for which they were created and to which they were appointed by God (for they had received free will from God),[207] while others acted wantonly[208] towards their own nature and their charge, that is, the ruler of this realm of matter and of the forms that are in it, and others that were in charge of the first firmament. Pray, realize that we tell of nothing without evidence, but expound what

the prophets[209] have declared. Well then, these angels
fell a-lusting after maidens and yielded to fleshly desires,
and he, the chief of them,[210] became heedless and wicked
in the administration of his charge. Thus by those that
went after maidens were the so-called giants begotten, and
it is no marvel that an account, though incomplete, of
the giants was told by the poets. Earthly wisdom differs
from that of the prophets as a likely tale does from the
truth; the one is earthbound and under the ruler of matter,
the other is from heaven.

We know how to tell many lies that look like truth.[211]

25. These angels, then, that fell from heaven, dwell
about our earth and sky and can no longer stretch upwards
into the regions that are above the heavens.[212] The souls
of the giants are those spirits that wander about the world,
and both classes are productive of motions, the spirits
producing motions akin to the natures they have received,[213] and the angels of such desires as those to which
they fell victims, while the ruler of this material world
guides and directs it in a manner opposed to the goodness
of God, as is evident from what happens:

Often has this thought come into my heart,
That either chance or a demon rules the affairs of men:
Contrary to hope and justice it drives some into exile,
Unmindful of God, while others are led to prosperity.

If good or ill success contrary to hope or desert left
Euripides speechless,[214] whose must be this administration
of things here below, of which one might say:

When we look upon all this, how can we say
That the tribe of gods exists, and why do we keep to laws?

This it was that made Aristotle say that things sublunary

were outside God's providence, though this eternal providence was evenly balanced in our regard,[215] whereas:

> The earth, whether she will or no, must put forth her grass,
> Fattening thence my flocks;[216]

and God's particular providence works towards truth and
not towards expectation for those worthy of it, while the
rest of nature is the object of providence in a general way
according to the law of reason.[217]

Now, since these spiritual impulses and influences from
the hostile spiritual power furnish the disorderly shocks
that move one man hither and another thither, singly
or in groups, in part or in common, in accord with their
kinship with matter or their response to the divine, from
within and from without,[218] therefore some men of no
little repute considered that all this visible world was not
put together by design but was the random product of
disorderly chance.[219] They failed to realize that there is
nothing disorderly or random about the materials that
go to make up this universe, but that each one of them was
made in reasonable fashion and thus they do not contra-
vene their appointed order. Man too is a well-ordered
being in his origin, with a nature which at the outset
presents one and the same kind of rationality in all. His
is a disposition[220] which according to his nature does not
transgress the law that is appointed for it, and a term of
life that remains steady and constant. Yet in his own indi-
viduality one man is harassed and dragged hither, another
yonder by the impulse of this thwarting ruler and his
attendant spirits, even though each man has the same
rational principle within.

26. Now these spirits are they that drag men towards
idols, engrossed in the blood from the altars,[221] even lick-

ing them round about, while the gods that catch the
popular fancy and give their names [222] to the idols were
originally men—as one can ascertain from their history.
That it is the evil spirits [223] who usurp these names one
can prove from the cult-operations in each case: some, for
instance, emasculate themselves, [224] as do the devotees of
Rhea; others, the devotees of Artemis, [225] make incisions
and gashes [and the Tauric goddess [226] puts strangers to
death]. I leave those who practise self-mutilation [227] with
knives and knuckle-bones to speak for themselves, and
all such forms of devilry. [228] It is not the work of God to
urge a man to what is against nature:

> For when the demon deviseth evil for a man,
> He damages his mind beforehand,

while God is ever perfectly good and eternally author of
good. [229]

The greatest proof that those who work through the
images are not the same as those whom they represent, [230]
is found in Troy and Parium. Troy has statues of Nerullinus [231]—a man contemporary with ourselves—and Parium,
of Alexander [232] and Proteus. [233] The tomb and statues of
Alexander are still in its market place. The statues of Nerullinus are normally just part of the city's decoration, seeing
that they are actually decorative, but there is one which
is supposed to give oracles and to heal the sick, and the
Trojans on that account offer sacrifice and anoint the statue
with oil and crown it with gold. The statue of Proteus
—the man who threw himself into the fire at Olympia,
as you know—is also said to give oracles, while to that of
Alexander:

> Paris ill-named, in form so fair, yet woman-struck—

public sacrifices are brought and feasts are held for it as

for a god who hearkens to prayers.[234] Now, is it really Nerullinus or Alexander or Proteus who produces these results for the statues, or the constitution of the material in them? The material is bronze: what can bronze do by itself, when it can be changed into another shape, as Amasis[235] did with the foot-bath in Herodotus? What more can Nerullinus and Alexander and Proteus do for the sick? For what the statue is now said to do, it did in the lifetime of Nerullinus and when he was sick himself.

27. What follows? The irrational and fanciful movements of the soul[236] in the field of opinion produce now one imagining, now another, some formed by material causes, others shaped and brought forth by themselves. The soul experiences this[237] most especially when it partakes of and commingles with the spirit of the material world,[238] gazing not upwards to the heavens and their maker but downwards to earthly things: in short, it becomes mere flesh and blood[239] and is pure spirit no longer. These irrational and imaginative movements of the soul produce the fancies of idol-madness. When a simple and docile soul, untaught and inexperienced in firm ways of thinking, without sight of the truth and unaware of the Father and maker of all, has impressed upon it[240] deceitful opinions about its own nature, the demons that rule matter, greedy for the fat of sacrifice and the blood from the altars, and being deceivers of men, take up these mistaken motions in the souls of the many and provide fancies that will trickle into their minds as if from the statues and shrines by manipulating them;[241] and any motion a rational soul, being immortal, may experience within itself that presages the future[242] or that heals present ills,[243] of this the demons enjoy the credit.

28. After the foregoing one must add something about

their names. Herodotus and Alexander,[244] son of Philip,
in his letter to his mother, say that they have learnt from
the worshippers themselves that these gods were once
men. Each of these is said to have had speech with the
priests in Heliopolis, Memphis, and Thebes. Herodotus
says: 'They made it clear that those whom the statues
represent were such as themselves, and quite different
from gods. Prior to their time, the rulers of Egypt were
gods who dwelt among mortals, and of these gods one
was always supreme. Later on, Horus, son of Osiris, ruled
Egypt (called by the Greeks Apollo). He overthrew
Typhon and was the last god-king of Egypt. Osiris is
Dionysus in the Greek tongue.'[245]

So this last and the others too were kings of Egypt.
The names of these gods passed from them to the Greeks.[246]
Apollo is son of Dionysus and Isis. Herodotus again
says: 'They say that Apollo and Artemis are children
of Dionysus and Isis, and that Leto was their nurse and
preserver.'[247] Those beings of heavenly origin they had
as their first kings; they took them to be gods, and their
wives along with them, partly through ignorance of
true piety towards God and partly through gratitude for
their rule: 'The male kine, if they are clean, and calves
the Egyptians sacrifice quite generally, but the females
are not allowed to be sacrificed. They are sacred to Isis.
⟨The statue of Isis indeed⟩ is that of a horned woman, in
the same way as Io is represented among the Greeks.'[248]

Who would be more deserving of credence in a tale
like this than father telling son in the line of tradition,
handing on priesthood and tale alike? It is not likely that
priests who took pride in their idols would lie in declaring
them once to have been men. Thus if Herodotus said that
the Egyptians spoke of their gods as if they were men, it

is not in any way right to disbelieve Herodotus as if he were a romancer when he says: 'I am not anxious to disclose the matters of divinity in the accounts I listened to; I will mention, however, the names of their gods.'[248a] And when Alexander and Hermes Trismegistus,[249] as he is called, and countless others too numerous to mention attribute an immortal[250] lineage to them, there is then no reason to prevent them being taken as gods, once they are kings. That they are men, the most learned of the Egyptians declare, for while calling earth, air, sun, moon, and the rest gods, they deem them to be mortal men and their graves to be temples. Apollodorus in his book *About Gods*[251] makes this clear. Herodotus says their sufferings are mysteries: 'The ceremonies for Isis in the city of Busiris I have already recounted. Men and women numbering many thousands take part in self-flagellation at the close of the sacrifice. But the manner of this flagellation it is not lawful for me to recount.'[252] If gods, they are immortal; if they are mourned for by flagellation, and their sufferings are mysteries, they are men. Herodotus again says: 'At Sais too, in the precinct of Athena, is the burial place of one whose name I do not think it right to mention in such a context.[253] It stands at the back of the shrine, covering the entire back wall. There is a lake there, girdled about with a stone parapet, in size about as large as the lake at Delos that is called the Hoop.[254] On this lake at night are reproduced the sufferings of the god, and these the Egyptians call mysteries.' Not only is the burial of Osiris shown but his embalming too: 'When a body is brought to them, they show the bearers various models of corpses made of wood and realistically painted. The most elaborate of these is said to be copied from him whose name in this context I do not think it right to mention.'[255]

29. Those learned among the Greeks for poetry and history say of Heracles:

> Feckless indeed, for he had no regard for the vengeance of the gods
> Nor for the table which he put before them;
> After the meal he slew him, even Iphitus.[256]

A being like that might well go mad, kindle a fire and burn himself to death. About Asclepius Hesiod says:

> The father of men and gods was wroth and with flashing thunderbolt
> From Olympus top he smote and slew the descendant of Leto,
> rousing up his anger against Phoebus,[257]

while Pindar says:

> Why, even wisdom is caught fast by greed,
> And gold flashing in his hand overswayed even such a one
> As this, with its promise of goodly reward;
> But speedily did the son of Kronos hurl down with both hands
> A bolt that cut short the breath of his lungs
> And all-glowing planted doom in him.[257a]

Either they are really gods, and then they would not behave like men about gold, saying:

> Gold, fairest present to men;
> Neither mother holds such delight, nor children,[258]

for the divine nature is in need of nothing and is above all coveting, nor would they die. Or else they were born as men, and are really wicked through their folly and are mastered by greed.

Why should I go on talking, instancing Castor and Pollux[259] or Amphiaraus, who though sons of men, born, as one might say, only the other day, are now revered as gods, when Ino[260] too is glorified as a goddess after her madness and the suffering that it caused?

Sea-wanderers will invoke her with the title Leucothea,

and her son:

Noble Palaemon will he be called by sailors.

30. If these, castaways hateful to the gods as they are, have had repute as gods, and if the daughter of Derceto, Semiramis,[261] a lascivious woman and a murderess, was taken to be the Syrian goddess—the Syrians reverence ⟨fish⟩ for the sake of Derceto[262] and doves for Semiramis's sake, and the miraculous story is in Ctesias that Semiramis was changed into a dove—what marvel if others are called gods by their contemporaries for their rule and despotism? The Sibyl, whom Plato also mentions,[263] says:

It was now the tenth generation of mortal men,
After the coming of the flood on the former generation;
Kronos was king, Titan and Iapetus too,
Worthy children of Ouranos and Gaia;
Men called them by their parents' names,
For that they were the first of humankind.[264]

Some for their strength, like Heracles and Perseus, others, like Asclepius, for their skill, received honours either from their subjects or from rulers themselves. Some got the name of gods out of fear, others out of reverence, while Antinous[265] had the good fortune to be named a god through the benevolence of your ancestors towards their subjects. Later on others took over the cult without any trial at all.

Cretans are ever liars, for thy tomb, O Lord,
Have the Cretans built, and yet thou art not dead.[266]

You believe, Callimachus, in the begetting of Zeus and disbelieve in his tomb. Thinking to overshadow the truth, you do in fact proclaim his death to ignorant men; and whereas on seeing the cave you are put in mind of Rhea's childbearing, on sight of his tomb you throw darkness over the story of his death, not knowing that the only everlasting being is the unbegotten God. Either the popular tales of the poets about the gods are unreliable and reverence for the gods is idle—for if the tales be lies, their subjects are non-existent;[267] or, if these births are true and these loves, these murders, thefts, maimings, and thunderbolts, they are now no more, having lost their godhead, since they came into being from nothing. What reason is there in accepting some tales and rejecting others from amongst those told by the poets to their renown? For those who wrote grandiloquently of them and caused them to be received as gods would not lie about their adventures.[268]

Our case has now been argued[269] to the best of our ability, if not as it deserves, to show that we are not atheists for reverencing as God the maker of this universe and the Word that comes from Him.

[Reply to the Second Charge]

31. But our enemies make a further false charge[270] against us, that we carry on impious banquets and unions among ourselves. They do this so as to be able to regard their hatred of us as reasonable and with the intent that by raising a scare they may detach us from our way of life, or make our rulers harsh and ill-disposed towards us by the sheer weight of their accusations. In this they play a game before those who are well advised of such tricks,

for from time long gone by, and not against us alone, it has been customary, by some kind of divine law and sequence, for evil to fight against the good. Thus Pythagoras [271] with three hundred companions was burnt by fire, Heraclitus was expelled from Ephesus, Democritus [272] from Abdera under the charge of madness; the Athenians, too, condemned Socrates to death. And just as they were no worse men [273] in the scale of virtue for this opinion of the multitude, [274] so we are not besmirched in our life of virtue by the unproven calumnies of a few, for we keep our reputation before God. Still I will answer these charges too.

I know that by what I have already said I have fully cleared myself; for you will realize, being without peers in wisdom, that those whose life has God for its rule will never come even to conceive the idea of the least transgression. This reputation of every one of us may be found blameless before Him [275] and free from every accusation. If we believed that this life here below was the only one to be lived, then it would be reasonable to suspect us of being enslaved by flesh and blood, subject to greed and passion and engaged in sins. But we know that God is present to all our thoughts and words, night and day, that He is light to all things and sees what is in our hearts. We believe that when we have departed from this life, we shall live another life in heaven better than this, not another earthly one. We shall then abide with God as heavenly spirits, not as fleshly creatures, even if we have bodies, and by His aid [276] shall be changeless and free from suffering in our souls. If we fall along with the rest of men, we shall live a much worse life there in fire. Again, God did not make us like sheep or cattle, and it is no bagatelle to Him if we should perish and be annihilated. It is not likely in view of all this that we should be minded to sin and to deliver ourselves up for judgment to the great Judge.

[REPLY TO THE THIRD CHARGE]

32. It is no marvel for them to fashion tales about us such as they relate about their own gods. They show the passions of their gods as mysteries. If they really thought promiscuous and unrestrained sexual intercourse wrong, they ought to hate Zeus[277] who begot himself children by his mother Rhea and his daughter Kore, and who took to wife his own sister; or Orpheus their poet who told of Zeus's wickedness and of his impieties worse than those of Thyestes,[278] though he too had intercourse with his daughter, wishing for kingly rule and revenge, and being bidden thereto by an oracle. But so far are we removed from promiscuity[279] that it is not allowed us even to look with passion upon another; for, as Scripture says, *he that shall look on a woman to lust after her, hath already committed adultery with her in his heart.*[280] God made our eyes to be a light to us, and we may not use them otherwise. For us a wanton glance is adultery, seeing that our eyes are made for a different purpose, and we are judged for what is no more than a thought. How then could such as ourselves fail to enjoy a reputation for chastity?

We have to reckon not with human laws[281] which one who had turned scoundrel might actually transgress with impunity, but our law is one of equality[282]—I pointed out in the beginning, my Lords, that our law came from God—and this law teaches us to have the same measure of justice for ourselves as for our neighbours. For this reason too we consider, according to age, some as sons and daughters; others we regard as brothers and sisters, and our elders we honour as fathers and mothers. We consider them then as brothers and sisters and give them other names of kinship, and therefore we set great store by keeping their bodies free from violation and corruption. Our law says furthermore[283]: 'If any man takes a second kiss for the motive of pleasure, etc. . . .'[284] We have thus to be so precise about the kiss, or rather the salutation,[285] since if any one of us was even in the least stirred to passion in thought thereby, God would set him outside eternal life.

33. Because of our hope of eternal life we despise the lesser goods of this life, even the pleasures the soul has herein. Each of us looks upon the wife he has married according to the laws we have laid down as one who will bear him children—no more.[286] The farmer sows his seed in the ground and waits for the harvest, not troubling to sow his land again the while. For us too the begetting of children is the limit of our indulging our passions, and one might find many amongst us, both men and women, who are growing old in virginity, their hope being to have greater fruition of God. If a life of virginity and self-deprivation recommends one to God, while to come nigh even to the thought of passion turns one away from God, then, if we shrink from the thought, much more will we flee from the deed. Our concern[287] is not a logomachy but a parade and school of deeds: either for a man to remain as he was brought into the world, or else to abide in one marriage and no more, for a second marriage is a fair-seeming adultery.[288] *Whosoever shall put away his wife,* Scripture says, *and shall marry another, committeth adultery.*[289] It does not allow him to divorce the one whose maidenhead he had,[290] nor to bring in another wife beside her.

One that robs himself of his first wife, even if she be dead, is a covert adulterer,[291] thwarting the hand of God—for in the beginning God made one man and one woman—and destroying the unity of flesh that was meant for the propagation of the race.[292]

34. Such as we are (for why[293] should I tell of secrets?), we accept the truth of the proverb that the harlot can teach the matron.[294] There are those who set up markets of harlotry and act as wicked procurers of the young for purposes of every base lust, not even refraining from boys, men with men working that which is base,[295] and in every way doing violence to such as are better-favoured and more noble in body, thus dishonouring God's created beauty (for there is no self-made beauty[296] on earth, but all comes down from the hand and mind of God). These men reproach us with those deeds which they have upon their own consciences and which they say their gods do,[297] and brag of them as noble and godlike. Adulterers and paederasts, they revile us who live in self-denial or single marriage. They live like fishes[298]: for these swallow whole what comes their way, the strong driving away the weak. This is the real feasting upon human flesh—that, whereas laws are established by yourselves and your predecessors most carefully for wholesome morality to prevail, they do violence to these laws, and even the governors that are sent out by you to the provinces are not able with their sanctions to control them.[299] We, on the other hand, are not allowed to withdraw ourselves when struck nor may we refrain from blessing when cursed.[300] It is not enough for us to be just (and justice is to give as good as we get); no, we must be good and long-suffering.

35. What reasonable man could call such men as us
6

murderers then? One cannot feed upon human flesh
without having killed someone. First, therefore, they are
liars in what they say;[301] secondly, if one of them is asked
if he witnessed what he asserts, no one is so shameless as
to say he did. Further, we have our slaves, some few, some
many, and so we cannot be without witnesses of our acts.
But none of our slaves has ever brought such false accusations as these against us.[302] Who can charge with murder
or cannibalism men who are known to be unwilling to
countenance even lawful homicide? Who is not held in
thrall[303] by armed contests and beast-fights, especially
when they are sponsored by yourselves?[304] But we consider the looking on at a murder to be nigh to murder
itself and forbid ourselves such spectacles. If then we do
not even look on at these shows (so as not to be under a
curse and to incur defilement), how can we be capable of
murder? Again, we call it murder and say it will be
accountable to God if women use instruments to procure
abortion[305]: how shall we be called murderers ourselves?
The same man cannot regard that which a woman carries
in her womb as a living creature, and therefore as an object
of value to God, and then go about to slay the creature
that has come forth to the light of day. The same man
cannot forbid the exposure of children, equating such
exposure with child murder, and then slay a child that
has found one to bring it up. No, we are always consistent,
everywhere the same, obedient to our rule and not masters of it.

36. When a man believes in the resurrection, how could
he make himself a tomb to receive those who will rise
again?[306] Indeed, the same man cannot believe in the
resurrection of his own body and then eat human bodies
as if they were not to rise again, nor can he expect the

earth to give up its dead and not to be asked himself to render up the dead he has buried within himself. Rather is it likely that those will not shrink from any shameless deed who think there will be no resurrection and no rendering of accounts for a good or evil life here below and who think that body and soul will perish together, being snuffed out like a flame. It is quite unreasonable to suppose that those will transgress even in the least detail who think that nothing will go unscrutinized before God and who are persuaded that the guilty body will share in the punishment due to the unbridled impulses and passions of the soul.

If a man deem it arrant nonsense[307] to talk of the body that has corrupted, decomposed, and disappeared coming together again, then we may be accused by unbelievers not of mischief but of folly. We wrong no man if we thus deceive ourselves with words. As a matter of fact, not only we but many philosophers[308] too claim that the body will rise again, so that it would be superfluous to argue the point here. We do not wish it to be thought that we are bringing in arguments that are beside the point—talking of the intelligible and the sensible and how they are put together, or preferring the disembodied to the embodied, or idea to sense (though sense gives us our first awareness) or describing how bodies come into being from what is bodiless[309] by a compounding of ideas while sensible reality depends on the ideal. It is quite possible, as Pythagoras and Plato said,[310] that when bodies dissolve into the elements out of which they were originally made, they can come together again out of the same elements.

[Conclusion]

37. Let this argument, however, about resurrection be put aside[311] for the present. But do you, most worthy in nature and upbringing, moderate, kind, and most deserving of high majesty, grant me your royal acquiescence now that I have dissipated all the charges and shown that we are God-fearing, modest, and restrained in our thoughts. Indeed, who are more worthy to obtain their requests than we, who pray[312] for your royal house that son may follow father[313] in most just succession of imperial rule and that your empire may receive prosperity and increase, with no rebellion anywhere? This is to our benefit too, *that we should lead a quiet and a peaceable life*[314] and render prompt obedience to all your commands.

THE RESURRECTION OF THE DEAD

[Exordium]

1. For every dogma and for every reasoned argument there is to be found some falsehood growing alongside the truth they contain.[1] This growth comes about not from the action of any natural cause in the subject matter itself nor yet from any formal principle in each dogma, but it is fostered by men who value illegitimate growths to the detriment of the truth.

One discovers this first of all from those who in olden times occupied themselves with thinking about these problems and about the difference that there was between themselves and their predecessors and contemporaries, and secondly, but not less so, from the very confusion that exists in the subject matter under dispute. Men like these have left no truth that was not overshadowed by falsehood, not the nature of God, not His knowledge and activity, nor the manifold consequences of the truths deduced[2] from these, nor the religious doctrine which we ourselves hold. Some indeed completely reject the truth about these things once for all, others go wandering off after their own opinions, while others again actually set out to doubt about what is manifest.

It is therefore necessary, I think, to address two arguments[3] to those who are in this perplexity, the one a plea for the truth, the other an exposition of the truth, the former being addressed to sceptics and doubters, the latter to those of good sense who receive the truth gladly. It is

79

the right thing therefore for those who wish to embark on this enquiry to look into the requirements of the situation in each case, and by this to shape the arguments that are to be produced, matching them with it and not losing sight of what is fitting and of what the situation in each case admits through a desire always to keep to the same exordium. For just as in demonstrations and scientific proof the exposition takes precedence over the plea, so, conversely, where the needs of a situation are more prominent, the plea undoubtedly precedes the exposition. A farmer[4] could not conveniently sow his seeds in a field when he had not previously cleared out the weeds and all that might be detrimental to the seed he was sowing for a crop; nor could a doctor conveniently inject any of the drugs needed for a sick body without previously having purged the mischief that was within or without having checked the onset of further trouble. Similarly, too, one who wished to teach the truth could not while lecturing about it convince a man in whose mind some false opinion was lurking as he listened and opposing all that was said. Having regard then to the needs of the situation, we too sometimes set the plea for the truth before its exposition; and in the present case it does not seem wholly useless to have regard to this necessity where the argument is concerned with the resurrection.

In a subject like this we find sceptics everywhere, others who are in doubt, and even amongst those who accept our first principles[5] some who are quite as perplexed as the doubters. What is most extraordinary, they fall into this predicament with no provocation to unbelief from the facts themselves and with no reasonable cause for their disbelief or perplexity.

2. We might put the matter thus. All unbelief that finds

lodgment in a man's mind, not rashly nor through some untested opinion but from a firm cause and with the assurance of truth itself, is then able to maintain a semblance of truth when the matter under challenge seems really incredible; whereas to disbelieve in what has no such character is what men do who have no sound judgment about truth. Therefore those who disbelieve in the resurrection, or who are in doubt about it, should not declare their views, giving utterance to untested opinions of their own or by saying what is gratifying to libertines.[6] Either they ought to regard the origin of the human race as dependent upon no cause at all—a position that it is only too easy to refute—or else, if they attribute the origin of all beings to God, they ought to examine the ground on which this dogma is based and show in regard to these that the resurrection is in no wise credible. This they will do if they contrive to show either that it is impossible for God or contrary to His will to unite together again bodies already dead, or even completely dissolved, and to bring them together again into the identical structure[7] of those same individuals. If they cannot show this, let them cease from their wicked unbelief and from blaspheming in most irreligious fashion. That they have not the truth when they say that it is impossible or against the will of God, will become clear from what I am about to say.

What is impossible for any agent is truly known to be such either from his ignorance of the effect to be produced or from his lack of power to produce in proper style the effect he knows. A man who was ignorant of one of the essential factors in the product would not be able to undertake or to effect at all that of which he was ignorant, while one who knew quite well what was to be produced, its

sources, and the manner of its production, but either completely lacked the power to produce what he knew or else
lacked sufficient power, would not set out to undertake
it at all, if he was wise and had regard to his own power.
If he undertook it without proper reflexion, he would
not achieve what he planned. Now God cannot be ignorant of the nature of the bodies destined to rise, in every
part and particle, nor of the destination of every portion
of what is dissolved, nor of what part of the element has
received that which has been released and returned to its
kindred element, even if to men it seem to be quite impossible to separate out that which has become once again
properly united with the common stock[8] of its element.
If He was not ignorant of the nature of the elements that
are to be constituted in being—out of which man's body
is to be formed—even before they enter severally into the
composition which is proper to them, and if He was not
ignorant of the parts of these elements from which He
was to take what was fitting for the composition of man's
body, then it is very clear that neither, after the complete
dissolution of the whole, will He be ignorant of the place
to which each part has gone that He took for the comple-
tion of each individual. As far as one can judge from the
present arrangement of affairs in our world, and according
to the judgment of men of the past,[9] it is the greater thing
to know beforehand what has not come to pass; while to
judge from God's majesty and wisdom, each task is natural
to Him, and it is just as easy for Him to know what has
gone into dissolution as to know beforehand what has
not yet come to pass.

[First Objection Countered]

3. What is more, the creation of each individual body shows that His power is sufficient for the resurrection of these bodies. For if He made human bodies and their constituents, even though they did not come into being at the first creation,[10] then even when they are dissolved in all kinds of ways, He will raise them up with the same ease, for the one is just as possible to Him as the other. Whether the first constituents come from a common matter, as some suppose, or the bodies of men come from the elements as from ultimate principles, or even from seed, it does not damage the argument. It is the act of one and the same power to give shape to what is customarily regarded by these philosophers[11] as shapeless matter, to arrange into many and varied patterns what was shapeless and disorderly, to unite into one the parts of the elements, to divide into many the seed that is one and simple, to make articulate what is not so, and to give life to that which has it not; and, on the other hand, to unite what has been dissolved, to raise up what has been laid low, to restore the dead to life and to change the corruptible into incorruption. It would then be the work of the same power, the same wisdom, and the same God to separate off what has been decomposed by the action of a multitude[12] of varied living creatures, such as are wont to swarm over such bodies and to sate themselves upon them, and to reunite it again in its proper portions and particles, whether it has gone into one of these creatures or into many and whether it has gone from them to others, or whether it has suffered dissolution along with the creatures in which it was, thus returning to its original constituents by the natural way of resolution into these. This indeed

it was that seemed most disturbing to some even of those famed for their wisdom, for they thought, I know not why, that the perplexities that are widely circulated about these questions were hard to dispel.

[Second Objection Countered]

4. Such men say,[13] for example, that many human bodies become, through drowning by shipwreck or in rivers, food for fishes; many of those who die in war or by some other hard fate or whim of circumstance lie unburied, are food for the first animals that approach. Bodies then, they say, are thus done away and their proper portions and particles pass after decay into a multitude of animals and are by digestion united to the bodies that thus feed upon them, so that the separating out of these becomes impossible. Then there is a further and more awkward predicament. The animals that feed upon these human bodies—such at least as are fit for human consumption—pass through the stomachs of men and are incorporated into the bodies of the men who eat them; and so the parts of those men who were preyed upon by beasts must of strict necessity go into the bodies of other men, the animals who fed upon them ferrying, as it were, the nourishment of which they partook into the men whose food they in turn became. Then, to heighten the air of tragedy, they bring in those who in madness or through famine dared to embark upon the eating of children, and those children who through stratagem were eaten by their parents, such as the Medic banquet [14] and the sad feast of Thyestes. They string together many such unusual disasters among Greeks and barbarians, and from all this they prove—as they think—that resurrection is impossible for

the reason that the same parts cannot rise again in two or
more bodies: either the former bodies will not be able
to achieve completeness, some of their parts now being
in other bodies, or if these parts are given up to their first
possessors, their later owners will be in want.

5. Such men seem to me not to realize the power and
wisdom of Him who made and governs this universe.
He arranged the food appropriate to the nature and kind
of each living creature and correspondent to it, and He
did not think it right that every natural kind should come
to be united and intermingled with every other corporeal
creature. Neither is He at a loss to separate things once
united, but enjoins upon the individual natures of created
things to do or to suffer what each was made for, and
He checks all other activities, forwarding each towards
all that He wishes and guiding it in that direction. What
is more, they have not examined the nature and capacity
of each of these creatures that eats or that is eaten. Surely
they would have recognized that not everything that may
be brought forward by pressure of external necessity is
suitable food for an animal. Some foods, as soon as they
encounter the folds of the stomach, are destined to be
broken up, either by retching and by evacuation, or dis-
posed of in some other way. Thus not even for a short
period do they undergo the first natural process of digestion, and still less [15] assimilation into the body of the eater.
Just so, it is not true that everything that is digested and
undergoes the first process of change is fully assimilated
by the organs that require nourishment, for some foods
have their nourishment extracted and passed on by the
stomach, while other foods are dissolved in the second
change, when digestion [16] takes place in the liver, and then
they assume another form which has lost the power of

nourishing. Again, it is not every product of metabolism in the liver that turns to nourishment for man, but the food dissolves into natural waste products, and the residual nourishment that is from time to time left in the organs to be nourished turns into something else according to the prevalence of an element which is either abundant or excessive and which is wont to change into itself or to dissolve all that comes near it.

6. There is thus a great variety of natures among all living animals and the natural food for each kind of living being varies with the body that is to be nourished. There are also three cleansings [17] and dissolutions in the feeding of each living being, and hence every element so alien as not to admit of assimilation in the form of nourishment must be either completely dissolved and drawn off to its appointed place, or it must change into something else. Next, when the quality of the food is naturally suited to the capacity of the animal that is to be fed, it must be passed through the natural process of straining, [18] and thus, being carefully purged by natural purgations, it must become a most excellent addition to the substance of the animal. This alone might one rightly call food, for it throws off every alien element that might do harm to the constitution of the creature that is being fed, and also all that excessive mass [19] that is introduced merely to cram the belly and to assuage the pangs of hunger. One can scarcely doubt but that this food is incorporated into the body that is to be nourished, being interwoven into and adapted to every part and portion thereof.

Now what is alien and unnatural food must dissolve quickly if it encounters [20] a stronger element, but will itself easily dissolve what it masters, turning into harmful humours and poisonous qualities, for it is bringing nothing that is proper to, or agreeable to, the body that is to be nourished. The chief proof of this is that as a result pain, danger, and death come upon many animals in their feeding, if, owing to their excessive appetite, something alien and poisonous is swallowed along with the food. This would cause the complete dissolution of the body fed, since it is true that animals are nourished by their natural food and wasted by its contrary. Thus, then, if there is a division of proper foods, corresponding to the difference of kind among animals, and if of this proper food not everything that is set before the animal nor any chance part thereof achieves conversion into the body that is being nourished, but only that part which has been purged by every process of digestion and completely changed in view of its incorporation into this particular body, thus being harmonized fully with the body it feeds, then it is quite clear that nothing unnatural could be incorporated into those bodies of which it is not the proper food designed for them, but must either pass through the belly before it produces any strange raw[21] juices or rottenness, or else it must lie there for a long time and produce pain or disease hard to cure, wasting along with itself the proper food of the body or even the flesh that is in need of nourishment. If it is ever dislodged by drugs or by better food or because it has been mastered by the power of nature, it is drained off with no small detriment, since it brought nothing that was agreeable to the body's natural disposition owing to its inability to coalesce with nature.

7. In fact, even if one were to agree that the food derived from these sources—let us so describe it for convenience' sake—though alien to nature, is absorbed, is broken up and changed into one of the hot or cold or

damp or dry elements, this concession would still be of
no advantage to our adversaries. Risen bodies are to be
put together again from their proper parts, whereas
none of the elements mentioned is a part, nor has it the
quality nor the position of a part, nor does it even remain
with the parts of the body that are being fed, nor does it
share [22] in the resurrection of those parts which are to rise
again, since in that state blood and phlegm, bile and breath
no longer make any contribution towards life. Bodies
will not then require the nourishment they once required,
for the use of what it fed on will be taken away along with
the desire for food and its metabolism.

Again, if someone were to suggest that the change
arising from such food went so far as to affect the flesh,
it would not even then be necessary for the animal's
flesh that had resulted from the metabolism of such food
again to function as a part in the building up of a man when
in its turn it was brought into the body of another man.
The flesh that receives increase does not always keep its
increments nor does the flesh that is incorporated into
another always abide and remain with its recipient, but
there is much change in both directions, physical and
mental labour carrying away some of what is received,
while pain, weariness, and disease cause the wastage of
other food, or else those distempers which result from
overheating or from a chill, while the fat membranes,
which store the nourishment and keep up their original
status, do not always share in the metabolism of the flesh
and of the soft fat. [23]

Since such things happen to all flesh, much more should
one expect to find it so with flesh that has been nourished
on improper food, so that it might at one time run to
excessive fatness and bulk from its intake, at another time

it might experience some form of vomiting and grow less from one or more of the causes mentioned above. That food alone would remain in the organs which was naturally designed for binding, sheltering, or warming, that which nature had chosen and had applied to those bodies whose natural life it helps to bring to perfection and whose labours it supports throughout life.

Since it is thus impossible to show the truth of what is alleged in favour of our opponents, either when our present investigations are judged in their proper light or when for the sake of argument we accept the principles they bring against us, it remains that human bodies can never enter into composition with other bodies of the same nature, not even when through a misapprehension men are deceived by sense perception and thus partake of other human flesh, nor where through hunger or madness they defile themselves with the flesh of their own kind. One must always suppose, that is, that we are right in denying the existence of anthropoid beasts,[24] or beasts with a nature in part human and in part bestial, such as the more daring of the poets are fond of imagining.

8. And then, why should we bother about those whose fate it is not to be eaten by animals but to receive burial in the earth as an honour due to their nature? Indeed, the creator has not assigned any animal as food for others of its kind, though it may naturally become the food of animals of other kinds. If on the one hand our opponents can show that human flesh has been assigned as food for other men, there will be no means of denying that cannibalism is according to nature,[25] just as much as any other natural proceeding, nor of preventing men who dare to say things like that from themselves feasting on the bodies of their nearest and dearest as being the food best fitted

for them, or from entertaining their best friends to the
same delicate fare. But if on the other hand it is impious
even to maintain such things and it is a horrid abomination
for men to feed on other men's flesh—a thing more
accursed than any other lawless and unnatural eating or
practice whatsoever—and if what is unnatural never turns
into nourishment for the parts and portions that need it,
and if again what does not turn into nourishment cannot
be incorporated into bodies which it was never intended
by nature to nourish, then human bodies can never be
incorporated into other human bodies that use them as
unnatural food, even should they by some unhappy fate
pass through the bowels of such men. Rather would such
food be withdrawn from the nutritive faculty and scattered
among those elements again from which it derived its
first embodiment, being united to them for as long a time
as is fitting, and separated again from them by the power
and wisdom of Him who couples the nature of each living
being with its appropriate powers. Thence will it be united
once again in its own nature, part with part, whether fire
has burnt it or water rotted it, whether wild beasts or
others have preyed upon it, or whether it has become
severed from the rest of the body and gone to destruction
before the rest. When these parts are reunited with each
other, they occupy the same positions in the bodily structure and constitution and they enjoy a resurrection to life
from being dead and completely dissolved. It is not for me
to dilate upon these facts any further: they receive the
assent of all who are not half-bestial themselves.

9. As there are many points of greater interest to the
present enquiry, I pass over the arguments of those who
appeal to the parallel with the works of man and man their
author, who is unable to renew them when they are

smashed or have decayed through lapse of time or in any other way have come to ruin. From the parallel with potters and carpenters [26] they try to show that God cannot be willing nor, if He is willing, can He be able, to raise up a body that has died or that has actually decomposed. They do not realize that in this way they show insolence towards God, just as much as the most reprobate do. They are putting on the same footing the capacities of beings entirely disparate, or rather they compare the natures of those who employ these powers, pitting art against nature.

To take such arguments seriously would be a matter hard to excuse from blame, for it is plain folly to argue against what is superficial and unfounded. It is far more probable and most in accord with the truth to declare that what is impossible to men is possible to God. If our argument shows by these probabilities [27] and by all the preceding investigation that this is possible, then it is clear that it is not impossible, and then, certainly, it is not outside God's will either.

[Third Objection Countered]

10. What is outside God's will is either unjust or unbecoming. Again, the injustice would be noticed either in the one who is raised from the dead or in someone else apart from him. But no one among those independent of the man himself and counted among the living suffers injustice; that is clear. Spiritual natures could not be wronged by the resurrection of men; such a resurrection does not hinder their existence; it does not harm them or affront them. Brute nature again and all that is inanimate does not suffer injury, for these will not remain in being

7

after the resurrection, and where there is no being there is no injustice. Even if one supposed that they actually remain in existence for ever,[28] they would not be wronged by human bodies being brought back to life. For if in their present state they suffer no wrong by yielding to man's nature that has need of them, and by bearing the yoke and all manner of slavery,[29] then surely much less will they suffer injustice if they become free from decay and in want of nothing and are no longer required to do this service for men but are freed from all slavery. Nor would they, if they enjoyed the gift of speech, accuse their maker because they are unjustly made inferior to men by their not sharing in the human resurrection. Where there is inequality of natures, the just judge does not assign the same end. Apart from these creatures that have no appreciation of justice, there is not even a charge of injustice possible.[30]

And certainly it cannot be maintained that any injustice can be found in regard to the man himself who is to be raised up: he consists of soul and body, and no injustice is sustained in either soul or body. No man in his right senses will say that the soul is wronged, for all unawares he will be casting out this present life along with that other. If a soul suffers no injustice now while it inhabits a mortal and passible body, much less will it suffer injustice when inhabiting one that is immortal and impassible. Nor is the body wronged at all, either. If now, when it, a corruptible thing, is associated with an incorruptible,[31] . . . does it suffer wrong? Again, one would not venture to say that it was a task unbecoming of God to reassemble and raise up the body which had corrupted. If the lesser work is not unbecoming, that is, to create a body that is mortal and passible, the greater work is certainly much less unbecoming, for it is a work of immortality and impassibility.

[RECAPITULATION]

11. If then by means of the first principles and by means of what comes after these each point of the enquiry has been cleared up, it is plain that the resurrection of decomposed bodies is a work that is possible to, within the free choice of, and befitting the creator. In this enquiry the objections have been shown to be false and the attitude of those who disbelieve it absurd. Is it really necessary to talk about the interrelation of these points one with the other and about their connexion with each other—if one can actually call it a connexion—as if they were matters divided off by some essential difference and it were not true that what is possible to God is within His free choice, and what is within His free choice is entirely possible and in keeping with the dignity of the chooser?

It is one thing to discourse about truth and another to plead its cause, as has been discussed in the foregoing chapters, which explained how these two lines of argument differ and when and against whom they are useful. Still there is nothing to prevent us making these and kindred ideas our point of departure once more, for the sake of giving assurance to all and showing the connexion between the foregoing and what is yet to come.

To discourse about truth is naturally the primary task, while the discourse on behalf of truth is the attendant of the former, pioneering for it and removing out of its way all that could hinder and check it. The discourse about truth is needed by all men for their safety and assurance, holding the primacy by its nature, its value, and its usefulness. Its nature is to provide knowledge of reality; its value is that it exists in and with those realities of which it is the go-between for us;[32] its usefulness is that it comes to be an ambassador of safety and assurance to all who have knowledge of it. The discourse on behalf of truth is inferior in nature and power, for it is a task of lesser degree to show up a lie than to lay hold of the truth; its value is less, for its strength lies in its opposition to false opinions—and false opinions are a second crop, produced by a second sowing and a gradual corruption.[33] Yet even in such circumstances as these it can be preferred and become more useful, by its removal and purging away of the unbelief that disturbs some minds and the uncertainty and false opinions of those who are approaching the truth. Each discourse leads to the same end, for he who shows up a lie and he who lays hold of the truth both have regard to edification. Not that they are absolutely one and the same. The one is necessary, as I said, to all who believe and who take thought for the truth and their own salvation; the other is for some people, sometimes, and in certain respects more useful.

This may suffice in a general way as a reminder of what has been already discussed. Now we must press on to our real object and show[34] the truth of the arguments for the resurrection: (a) from the motive itself according to which and because of which the first man came into being, and his progeny too, even if they did not actually share the manner of his creation, (b) from the nature of all mankind, (c) from the judgment of the creator about these men, according to their length of life and mode of acting —a judgment which one cannot fail to regard as just.

[Argument from the Motive of Creation]

12. This is the argument from motive, that we should determine whether man was made simply for no purpose at all or for some purpose. If for some purpose, was it that he should live when born and remain in the nature which he had, or be at the behoof of another? If at someone's behoof, is it at that of the creator Himself, or at that of someone allied to Him and by Him deemed worthy of greater regard? If we make an examination of the most general principles, we find that no one who is right-minded and who is stirred by the power of reason to accomplish anything at all acts at random in anything [35] where free choice is exercised. He acts either for his own advantage or at the behoof of another for whom he has some regard or for the sake of the product of his action itself, moved by some natural bent and yearning for its production. [36]

For instance—to explain by means of an example, to make clear what is involved—a man makes a house for his own need; but for oxen, camels, and other animals, of which he has need, he makes the shelter that is suitable for each, not apparently for his own need, but on the long view for that very need, while on the shorter view he acts on behalf of those animals with which he is concerned. Children too he gets for himself, not for his own need nor for the sake of anything belonging to him, but to secure that, as far as possible, his offspring should persist in being, [37] consoling himself in this way by the succession of children and descendants for his own mortality, thinking thus to immortalize [38] what is mortal. This is what men do. Now God did not create man for no purpose at all. He is wise, and no work of wisdom is devoid of all purpose. Nor did

He make him for His own need. He is indeed entirely free from all needs, and to a Being in need of nothing at all none of His creatures could contribute anything for His own need. Again, He did not make man for the needs of any other of His creatures, for none among the creatures that use reason and judgment, whether of higher or lower degree,[39] has been or is created for the need of another, but for the individual life and persistence in being of itself. Reason indeed cannot find any need as the cause of man's creation. The immortals are free from every need and never require from men a contribution to their being, while irrational creatures are naturally dependent and serve the needs of man in whatever way nature has arranged for them,[40] not being themselves fashioned to make use of men. It was never right, nor is it, that the dominant and principal being should serve the needs of what is inferior, nor should reason serve the irrational that is unfit to bear command.

Thus, since man was created neither in vain nor without cause—for nothing made by God lacks a cause in the mind of the maker—nor yet for the need of the creator nor of any of His creatures, it is plain that God made man, in the first and most general aspect of the matter, for Himself and for His goodness' and wisdom's sake, that was to be made manifest upon the face of all His handiwork.[41]

In the aspect that most nearly concerns creatures themselves, He created man for the sake of the life of man the creature, a life not to be kindled for a brief space and then snuffed out. Such a fleeting mode of life He did impart to crawling things, I suppose, and to winged things and those that swim, or, in more general terms, to all irrational creatures; but to those who bear in themselves the image[42] of the creator, whose nature involves the possession of mind and who partake of rational judgment, He has set apart an eternal existence, that knowing their maker and His power and wisdom, and being guided by law and justice they may share in an undisturbed, everlasting existence along with those helps by which they mastered their preceding life, though they were in frail and earthy bodies. For, firstly, anything which is created for the sake of another, when that other ceases to be, can itself be reasonably expected to cease from being; it would not be likely to remain bereft of its reason for being, for such idle creatures have no place in the universe made by God. Then again, what is created for the sake of its own life and its existence according to nature, could never admit of any cause completely annihilating its being, because the cause itself would be comprehended within the nature and would be regarded only in the aspect of one that exists.[43] Now if the cause is regarded as remaining in being for ever, then the living creature likewise must by all means be kept in being, acting and being acted upon naturally, with each of its constituent parts contributing its proper share. The soul, too, remains in an equable existence proper to it by nature and undertakes its natural tasks;[44] that is to say, it is by nature appointed to govern the instincts of the body and to judge and estimate by suitable canons and measures the stimuli that occur. As for the body, it is set on by nature to what is proper to it and undergoes its destined changes, along with its other changes in age, appearance, and size, finally undergoing resurrection. This is indeed a kind of change and the last of such changes, a change for the better[45] in all those who remain in existence still at that time.

13. Let us take heart at these considerations, no less than at what has come to pass already, and let us examine

our own nature. We put up with the needs and wastage
of this life as one suited to the present time, and we have a
firm hope in our permanence in immortality. We do not
fabricate this hope idly from human testimony, beguiling
ourselves with fraudulent hopes,[46] but we have given
credence to a surety that can never lead us astray—the
mind of our maker, according to which man was made of
an immortal soul and a body, was endowed with intelligence and with a law implanted in him that would safe-
guard and protect the creator's gifts to him that were
suited to a conscious being with a rational life. We are
well aware that God would not have created such a living
being and endowed him with all the gifts suited to permanence, if He did not want His creature to be permanent.[47] If then the creator of all made man to share in a
conscious life and, when he had become the witness of
His majesty and all-embracing wisdom, to abide for ever
in the contemplation of these, according to the divine
purpose and the nature he had received, then the reason
for his coming to be guarantees his permanence for ever,
and his permanence guarantees his resurrection, for without this he would not be permanent *as man*.[48]

Thus it is clear from what has been said that by the
reason for creation and the purpose of the maker the
resurrection is clearly proved. Such being the reason for
which man has been brought into the world, it would
seem natural to consider next the argument which depends upon these ideas by a natural necessity or by a strict
logical sequence.[49] The nature of the men who have been
created comes next in our enquiry after the cause of their
creation. Their creator's just judgment upon them comes
next after the nature of the men created, just as the end of
life follows upon all these. Now that we have completed

the first part of the enquiry, we must next examine the
nature of man.

[Argument from the Nature of Man]

14. The demonstration of true dogmas—or of those
that are anyhow put forward for examination—if it is
to confer an unshakeable guarantee upon what is said,
has no outside source nor does it rely upon what some
men think or have thought, but comes from the universal
and natural notions or from the logical dependence[50] of
conclusions upon axioms. It is either a question of axioms
—and then one needs do no more than put men in mind of
them[51] to excite the natural notion—or else it is a question
about natural conclusions from axioms and logical implication, and then one needs to observe the right order in such
things, showing what truly follows from the axioms and
initial positions, at the same time not disregarding truth
and its guarantee,[52] nor confounding things which nature
has appointed to be distinct nor yet disturbing the natural
sequence. It is then right, I think, for those who are in
earnest about such matters and who are ready to make
a prudent judgment whether the resurrection happens
or not, first of all to make a thorough examination of
the cogency of those arguments which contribute to
this demonstration and to see what place each holds,
which of them is first, which second or third, and which
last.

When this examination is made, one must put first the
reason of man's creation, that is, the purpose the creator
had in making man, and then immediately connect with
this the nature of man created—not because it occupies
a secondary place, but because we cannot pass judgment

upon both at the same time, however much they are linked together and furnish arguments of the same cogency for our subject. When the resurrection is clearly demonstrated by means of these arguments which are primary and have their origin in creation itself, one can obtain a proof of it in no way inferior from the argument of providence. I mean the argument from the rewards and punishments due to each individual man in a just judgment and from the end of human life.

Many divide up the argument, when making their division of arguments for the resurrection, by putting all the weight on the third argument alone and think there must be a resurrection because of the judgment. This is shown to be clearly false from the fact that all dead men will rise again, but not all the risen will be judged.[53] If the fact of the judgment were the sole and sufficient reason for the resurrection, then those who had never done wrong, that is to say, those who had kept on the right path, ought not to rise at all—children, for instance, that are still quite young.[54] But since they will admit that all rise again, even those who die in infancy, it is not true that the resurrection happens primarily because of the judgment, but because of the creator's purpose and the nature of created things.

15. The reason that is derived from a consideration of the origin of man is, even by itself, sufficient to demonstrate that a resurrection ensues by natural sequence upon the dissolution of the body. All the same, it is perhaps right not to hold oneself aloof from any of the arguments proposed, but in agreement with what has been said to manifest to those who cannot themselves discern such things the grounds for each of the lines of deduction, and especially the nature of the men who have been created, for this

leads to the same concept and provides the same guarantee for the resurrection.

If, quite generally, every instance of human nature is constituted by an immortal soul and the body that is united with it at birth, and if God has decreed such an origin, such a life and existence, neither for the soul by itself nor for the body in isolation, but for the men who are compounded of the two, intending that from the time that they are united and commence to live they should pass through life and come to one and the same appointed end, then it needs must be that the whole class of beings derived from them [55] be referred to the one end, seeing that of body and soul there is in every case one being compounded that undergoes all bodily and spiritual experiences, and acts in performance of whatever calls for judgment of sense or reason. Thus all concur throughout to form one harmony and concordance: man's creation, his nature, his life, his works and sufferings through life, and the end that is appointed for his nature. But if there is one harmony and concord of the whole living being, both of those things that spring from the soul and of those that result from the body, there must be one end appointed for all alike. Now this end will be truly one if the being whose end it is remains the same in its constitution; the living being will clearly remain the same if all that constitutes its parts remains the same; and the parts will remain the same with the same ingression [56] into their individual union, if what is dissolved comes into being again to make up the living creature.

Thus the constitution of man in self-identity shows that the resurrection of bodies that have died and have been dissolved must follow of necessity, for without it the same parts would not be united to one another, nor would the

same nature of man be reconstituted. But if mind and reason are given to men for the discernment not only of
substances but also of the goodness, wisdom, and justice
of the giver, then it must follow that where those objects
abide for which reasoning judgment has been granted,
the judgment that is exercised upon them must also abide,
and this cannot abide without the nature that receives it
and the objects upon which it is exercised. Now it is man
who receives ideas [57] and reason, not the separate soul.

So man then, who is constituted of both body and soul,
must abide for ever. This he cannot do without a resurrection, for if the resurrection does not take place, the nature
of man as man will not abide; and if his nature abides not,
then to no purpose has the soul been attuned [58] to the
needs of the body and to its experiences, and in vain has
the body been fettered in its winning what it strives for
by the bridle rein of the soul and curbed by it. Vain too,
is the mind, vain prudence and the expectation of justice,
the practice of every virtue, the enactment of laws and their
codification, and, in short, all beauty that is in man and
through man, [59] and, still more, the creation and nature of
man himself. But if this lack of purpose is excluded from
all the works of God throughout and from all the gifts
that are given by Him, then perforce must the permanence
of the body be of equal duration with the unending existence of the soul in one proper human nature.

16. Let no one be surprised that we name a life that is
interrupted by death and decay a permanence. Let him
consider that this word bears more than one sense, [60] that
permanence has more than one measure, and that not even
is there one single nature among the things that abide. If
then each thing that abides enjoys this permanence according to its own nature, one would not expect to find in the

case of those that are simply incorruptible and immortal, a permanence that was entirely on the same footing. The reason is that the substance of a superior being is not levelled down to that of those which represent a declension from its reality. Nor is it right in the case of man to look for a splendidly equable and unruffled permanence, since the superior beings were made immortal and permanent from the start by the mere will of their creator, while men have indeed from their creation an unshaken permanence in soul, but in body they receive incorruption as an addition after change.

Our account of the resurrection involves this. We look to the resurrection, putting up with the dissolution of the body as consequent upon a life that is involved in needs and decay, and we hope for permanence [61] in incorruption after this life. We do not match our death with that of unreasoning animals nor our human permanence with that of the immortals, in order not to fall into the error unawares of equating human nature and life with beings that are unfit objects of comparison.

It is not right to be disturbed at this, when some inequality is observed in human permanence, nor even [62] to refuse to admit the resurrection just because the separation of the soul from the body or the dissolution of the body into its proper parts interrupts the continuance of life. The naturally-produced slackening of the senses and physical powers in sleep also seems to interrupt the life of conscious awareness, when men fall asleep and in a manner come back to life again by regular intervals of time: yet we do not refuse to call this a living existence. That is the reason, I suppose, why some call sleep death's brother,[62a] not making out their pedigree as they were begotten from the same sire and of the same kindred, but because a similar experience befalls the dead and those that sleep, in respect of their quietness and lack of perception of what is present or taking place, and even of their own life and existence. If then we do not refuse to call this human existence the same life, so full of anomalies from birth to dissolution and interrupted as it is by all that we have described, neither ought we to refuse the name of life to what is beyond [63] the dissolution, since it brings with itself the resurrection, even if for a time it is interrupted by separation of the soul from the body.

17. This human nature from its origin and by the will of its creator has this anomaly allotted to it, that its life and permanence should be irregular, being interrupted now by sleep, now by death, and by the changes that come with the successive ages of man, the later stages of which are not clearly foreseen during those that come earlier. Who would have thought—if he had not learnt it by experience —that in uniform [64] and undifferentiated semen there were enclosed such a variety of powers [65] of every sort and strength, with tissues in readiness for differentiation and consolidation; I mean bones, nerves, and cartilages; yes, and muscles, too, and flesh, intestines, and the other parts of the body? It is impossible to see any of these while the semen is yet liquid, nor does one see in infants any of the qualities of grown-ups, nor in adult age those of men who are ageing, nor in these the qualities of the senile. All the same, even though some of these stages exhibit but feebly and others not at all the natural sequence and the changes that are proper to the nature of man, those whom malice or indifference does not blind in their judgment of these things know that there must first come the depositing of the seeds, then their articulation into proper parts and divisions, the coming forth of the progeny, the first

stages of growth, then adolescence, the slackening of the
physical powers until old age, and finally the breakup of
bodies that are worn out. Now in these conditions the
semen does not bear inscribed in it the shape or growth
of man, nor does human life bear inscribed its dissolution
into component elements; but the train of natural happen-
ings [66] provides a guarantee for those facts which would
otherwise have no guarantee from the phenomena [67] themselves. Still more is this the case when reason, seeking the
truth from the natural sequence of events, guarantees the
resurrection, for reason is a surer and stronger guide than
experience [68] in the guaranteeing of the truth.

[Argument from Rewards and Penalties]

18. The arguments we have just now put forward for
consideration as a guarantee of the resurrection are all of
the same kind, springing from the same root idea, for their
first principle is the origin of mankind by creation. Some
of these arguments derive their cogency from the first
principle from which they come, while others derive it
from the providence of God in our regard, for they are
dependent upon the nature and life of man. The reason
according to which and on account of which man came
into being, jointly considered with the nature of man,
derives its force from the fact of creation, while the argument from justice, [69] according to which God is going to
judge men who have lived good or evil lives, draws its
strength from their end. Men spring forth from the creative
hand of God, but depend chiefly upon His providence.

Now that the former argument has been exposed by
me according to my ability, it is appropriate to undertake
the second demonstration also, that is, by means of the

rewards and punishments due to each man in just judgment and from the end of human life. Here one must first consider what is by nature primary and examine the account of the judgment, premising this only, out of regard for the first principle proper to the present subject matter and for right order: (a) that those who accept God as the creator of this universe must ascribe to His wisdom and justice the guardianship and oversight of all that comes to pass—at least if they are to be consistent in their first principles; and (b) that, engaging in such considerations, they should reckon that nothing in heaven nor on earth is beyond the reach of guardianship and forethought, but should recognize that the care of the creator runs through small and great, visible and invisible all alike. Clearly all things created need the care of their creator, each one privily according to its nature and destiny.

To propose at this point a catalogue of the kinds of creature, properly divided, or of the ends suited to each, would be a useless parade of knowledge. But man anyhow, the subject of our present enquiry, being needy, must have food; being mortal, must have progeny; being reasonable, must have justice. Each of these belongs to man by nature: he needs food for his life, he needs progeny for the permanence of his kind, and he needs justice for the fair distribution of food and progeny, and so it will be admitted that as food and progeny concern the whole man, justice must bear upon the whole man too, that is, the whole man composed [70] of body and soul, and such a man must become liable to receive reward and punishment for all his deeds. Now just judgment apportions justice for his deeds to the whole man, and the soul alone should not receive the wage for what it has done in the body's company—for the soul taken by itself is without engagement[71] in the excesses that occur in bodily pleasure, in feeding, or in nurture; nor should the body alone be rewarded—for the body by itself is outside the scope of reason and justice.

The whole man, therefore, composed of body and soul, receives justice for each of his acts. But our enquiry discovers that this does not happen in this life, for here in this life true deserts are not observed, when many atheists and consummate villains go to the end of their lives without experiencing hardship; while again those who show that their life is lived in the practice of all virtue live in pain, in insults, in calumnies, outrages, and all kinds of misfortune. Nor does it happen after death, for there the whole man no longer exists, when the soul is separated from the body and the body itself scattered again into those elements from which it came, keeping nothing any longer of its former beauty and vivacity or even the memory of its deeds. The inevitable conclusion is obvious to all, that this scattered and corrupting body must put on incorruption, as the Apostle said,[72] so that when the separate and completely scattered elements are reunited and what was dead has come to life again in the resurrection, each man may receive justice for what he did in the body, whether good things or ill.

19. With those who admit the providence of God[73] and accept the same first principles as ourselves, and then somehow fall away from their own hypotheses, one might employ such arguments as these; yes, and many more than these, if one wished to enlarge upon what is here said briefly and in a hasty fashion. But with those who disagree about first principles, perhaps it would be well to substitute another point of departure in preference to these principles. One could join with them in their doubts

about the opinions they hold and take part with them in enquiries such as this: Is it true now, that the whole of human life and the whole course of man's existence has been disregarded [74] once for all and that a dense mist has engulfed the earth, hiding in silence and contempt men and their works? Or is it much more secure to reckon that the maker presides over His works, oversees all that is or ever shall be, and judges of deeds and plans? If there should never be a judgment upon man's deeds, men will be no better off than the brutes. Nay, they will fare worse than these, by holding their passions in subjection and taking thought for piety and justice [75] and the other virtues, whereas the life of a beast, even a wild beast, is best of all. Virtue is made folly, and the threat of judgment will raise a broad laugh. The high good is to foster every pleasure. Of all such the common creed [76] and one principle is that dear to the wanton and licentious—*Let us eat and drink, for tomorrow we shall die,* for some hold that such a life does not end in pleasure either, but in a complete insensibility. [77]

If, on the other hand, the creator of men does take some thought for His creatures and a just judgment is ever held of man's good or evil life, this must be [78] while they still live who have followed after virtue or vice, or else after death, when they are in a state of separation and dissolution. But one cannot find that in either case the just judgment is carried out, for in this life the zealous do not bear away the reward for virtue, nor the wicked the wages of sin. I do not wish to emphasize that so long as the nature we now possess remains, our mortal frame is unable to bear the condign punishment for the greater number of transgressions or one convenient to the more serious crimes. The robber, for instance, or the private despot or tyrant who has thousands and thousands of lawless slayings to his account could not pay the penalty for these by a single death. One who has never had a true thought about God, who has lived in all wantonness and blasphemy, despising religion, breaking the laws, debauching boys and women alike, unjustly destroying cities, burning houses with their inhabitants, ravaging fields, thereby making away with villages, tribes, or even a whole race; how could he in a mortal body render condign satisfaction for all these?[79] Death would rob him of his deserts, and his mortal frame would be inadequate to satisfy for even one of his crimes. Judgment according to desert cannot then be found in this life nor yet after death.

20. Either death is the complete extinction of life, where the soul goes into dissolution along with the body and corrupts along with it, or else the soul abides by itself without breakup, scattering, or corruption, while the body is dissolving and corrupting with no memory of what it has done nor any perception of what the soul is experiencing. If the life of man is to be completely extinguished, then manifestly there will be no reckoning in the case of men who are not living, no judgment of those who have lived virtuously or viciously; but the feats of wicked living will come back on to the stage[80] of life one after another, and the swarm of unreasonable consequences derived from them, and—head and front of this wickedness—disbelief in God.

But again, if the body corrupts and each part returns to its appropriate element, while the soul remains by itself incorrupted, there will be no place even then for its being judged, since justice would not be present at such a judgment. It is in no way lawful to expect any judgment to come from God directly or indirectly at which justice is not present. Now justice is not present at a judgment where the doer of just or wicked deeds is no longer in existence; and it was man who was the doer of each of the actions of the life that is being judged, not soul alone. To conclude in brief: such an account of the world would in no wise stay within the limits of justice.

21. When right actions are being rewarded, the body will clearly be wronged, since it was the soul's partner in the labours involved in virtuous action, but it is not its partner in the reward for its righteous conduct. While the soul will often be excused for some of its misdeeds by reason of the body's deficiency and needs, the body will not benefit from the partnership in righteous acts for the sake of which it shared in the toil that went with life. Furthermore, when faults are being judged, justice for the soul is not kept if the soul alone[81] pay the penalty for what wrongs it did when the body hindered it or drove it on towards bodily desires and motions, the body sometimes seizing it and carrying it along with itself, sometimes using still more violent urgings, or at other times by collusion[82] bringing it to show kindness and a desire to preserve bodily well-being.

Surely it is unjust for the soul to be judged by itself[83] for acts where by its own nature it has no appetite, no impulse, no stirring, such as wantonness, violence, or covetousness and the wrongs that follow upon these. The greater part of these ills arise from men not mastering their obstructive passions, and the obstruction is caused by the body's deficiency and needs, and by concern for this and attempts to deal with it. For this is the cause of all possession of property—and, still more, its use—of marriage and of actions concerned with the production of life,[84] in which and in regard to which bad conduct and its opposite are to be seen. How then is it just that where the body is the first beneficiary[85] and drags the soul onwards to sympathy with and partnership in the deeds to which its instincts drive it, the soul should be judged? How is it just that the yearnings and enjoyments, yes, and the fears and griefs to which all unmeasured activity is liable, should take their rise from the body, while the resultant transgressions and the penalties for them should be visited upon the soul alone that did not ask for anything like this, nor yearn for it, nor fear for it, nor undergo by itself any other human passion?

If on the other hand we suppose that these passions are not proper to the body alone but to man as such,[86] we shall indeed be correct in our description, in so far as man's life is one life derived from both, but we shall certainly deny that these belong to the soul also, as long as we regard its own proper nature in a clear light. Entirely without need of food of any kind, it could never have yearned for things which were in no way necessary for its being, nor could it have gone in search of those things it was never meant to enjoy. It could not have grieved for lack of money or possessions, for they have nothing to do with it. Seeing besides that it is superior to corruption, it fears nothing at all as being likely to corrupt it. It fears not hunger nor disease, nor maiming nor disfigurement, neither fire nor sword, since it cannot suffer any harm or pain from these, for bodies and bodily properties cannot affect it at all. Now if it is absurd to attribute the passions to the soul in an exclusive sense, it is certainly unjust and unworthy of the judgment of God to visit upon the soul alone the transgressions that come from passion and their due chastisement.

22. In addition to the above, is it not absurd that, while

virtue and vice cannot even be conceived as separate in the soul alone—for virtues, we know, are the virtues of men and the vices that oppose them are likewise not the property of the soul in isolation and apart from the body—yet the reward or punishment for these is to be visited upon the soul alone? How could a man really conceive courage or stubborn endurance to exist in the soul alone, when it has no fear of death or wounding or lopping, nor of loss, ill-treatment, or pain arising out of these, nor of the consequent suffering? How could he really conceive continence and restraint, when no lust draws it on to food or intercourse or to the other pleasures and delights, and nothing from within disturbs it and nothing from without inflames it? Or how conceive prudence, when the choice what to do or not to do, accept and reject, is not submitted to it, or rather when there is in it no movement at all or natural desire towards anything that is to be done? How, in fine, can justice towards each other be a natural property of souls, or towards any other similar or dissimilar being? They have no means nor stimulus nor way of rendering equality either of deserts[87] or of proportion to anyone, apart from the honour due to God; nor have they any stirring or motion to use what is their own or to refrain from what is another's,[88] for use and restraint are seen in respect of natural goods and of those which are made for use,[89] while the soul is in need of nothing, and it is formed by nature to use nothing whatever, and therefore the so-called private enterprise[90] of the parts can find no place in a soul that is thus constituted.

23. Furthermore, the most absurd thing of all is that the laws established apply to men, while the reward for lawful and unlawful acts affects the soul alone. If the same subject who received the laws received also the recompense of

his transgressions according to justice, and that subject
was man, and not the soul by itself, it would be right for
man and not the soul by itself to submit also to retribution
for his misdeeds. In fact, God did not issue a decree to
souls that they were to keep away from what did not concern them, such as adultery, murder, robbery, pillage, dishonouring of parents, and in general from every passion
leading to injury and injustice to one's neighbour. The
command, *Honour thy father and mother*, is not designed to
suit souls alone, for such names do not apply to them.
Souls do not beget souls and thus earn for themselves the
title of father or mother,[91] but men beget men. Therefore
likewise, the command, *Thou shalt not commit adultery*,
could not have been spoken to souls, or even properly
thought of in their regard, for in souls there is no difference
of male and female,[92] no aptitude for sexual intercourse
and no desire for it. Since there is no appetite of that
nature, it is impossible for there to be intercourse, and
where there can be no intercourse, there cannot be the
lawful intercourse of marriage. If there is no lawful intercourse, there cannot be unlawful—neither the lust after
another's wife, nor the intercourse which constitutes
adultery.

   Again, it is not natural for souls to be forbidden theft
or the desire for the goods of another. They do not de-
mand those things, through the need of which, either
through natural deficiency or passing need, men will rob
and steal gold, silver, cattle, or other things useful for
food, shelter, or advantage .Whatever is an object of desire
to deficient beings, as being useful to them, is by nature
useless to an immortal.

   We may leave the fuller examination of these things to
those who are anxious to scrutinize details, or who will

engage in spirited debate with those who differ from them.
This present discourse is sufficient for us and arguments in
agreement with it which guarantee the resurrection; it
would not be timely to continue lecturing upon the same
points [93] at greater length. We have not made it our aim to
omit nothing that could possibly be said on the subject,
but to show in a summary way to those here assembled
what one ought to think about the resurrection and to
adapt to the capacity of the audience the considerations
that bear upon the argument.

[Argument from the End of Man]

24. Now that the topic proposed has been to some extent
examined, it remains to consider the argument from the
final cause. It has already been outlined in the foregoing,
but it needs just so much attention and amplification as
will free me from the implication of leaving unrehearsed
any of the points mentioned above and thus of damaging
my original proposal or the division of the matter laid
down at the outset. For this reason and because of com-
plaints that might be made on this score, it may be well
just to make this clear, that every natural thing and every
artefact must have its own end. [94] The common understanding of all men teaches us this, and what we see before
our eyes bears witness to it. We see, surely, that there is
one end for farmers [95] and one for doctors, that plants
which grow in the earth have one end, and animals which
are nourished upon it and procreated in a natural series
have another. If this is clear, and a natural end must perforce belong to natural or artificial powers and to the
activities they put forth, then it is strictly necessary that
the end of man, since it is the end of a distinctive nature,

should be raised above that of the generality. It would simply not be right to suppose the same end for beings which lack the judgment of reason, and for those which act according to an innate law of reason and enjoy a rational life and justice.[96] A state of freedom from pain could not be an end for them,[97] for they would share that with those that are entirely without perception;[98] nor yet can it be the enjoyment of those things which feed and delight the body nor a surfeit of pleasure. Must the brutish life bear the primacy, and the life of virtue lack an end? For that is, I suppose, the proper end of oxen and cattle, and not of men who have an immortal soul and rational judgment.

25. Nor again is there happiness for the soul separated from the body. We have not been examining the life or the end of the two constituents which make up man, but that of the compound, man. For such is every man who shares this life of ours and of a life like this there must be some proper end. If now the end is that of the whole man,[99] and for the reasons already given many times over this cannot be discovered in the life here below, nor yet when the soul comes to be separate (since a man cannot be said to exist as such when the body is dissolved or completely scattered, even though the soul remain by itself): then by strict necessity the end of man must be found in some other condition of the whole man, who yet remains the same man.

As this is a necessary consequence, there must certainly be a resurrection of bodies whether dead or even quite corrupted, and the same men as before must come to be again.[100] The law of nature appoints an end not absolutely, nor for some men or others, but for those very same men who lived in a previous existence, and it is impossible for the same men to come together again if the same bodies are not given back to the same souls.[101] Now the same soul cannot recover the same body in any other way than by resurrection. When this happens, the end befitting the nature of man is really achieved. One would not be far wrong in describing the end of a life of understanding and reasoning judgment as a perpetual and inseparable companionship [102] with those realities for which the natural reason is principally and primarily adapted, in the unceasing and exultant contemplation of our Benefactor,[103] and of all that He has decreed, in spite of the fact that the majority of men, having yielded excessively and easily to the pleasures of this life, remain for ever without a share in that bliss. The great number of those who fail to reach their appointed end does not annul [104] the general enjoyment of it: the examination into such matters differs in each one, as does also the reward or punishment for a good or evil life [105] that is made proportionate to each several man.

NOTES

LIST OF ABBREVIATIONS

ACW   Ancient Christian Writers (Westminster, Md.—London 1946–)

CAH   Cambridge Ancient History (Cambridge 1923–39)

CIL   Corpus inscriptionum latinarum (Berlin 1863–)

DACL   Dictionnaire d'archéologie chrétienne et de liturgie (Paris 1907–)

DCB   Dictionary of Christian Biography and Literature (London 1911)

DTC   Dictionnaire de théologie catholique (Paris 1903–50)

EC   Enciclopedia cattolica (Rome 1949–54)

FHG   Fragmenta historicorum graecorum (Paris 1841–70)

IG   Inscriptiones graecae (Berlin 1873–)

JTS   *Journal of Theological Studies* (1899–)

LSJ   Greek-English Lexicon, by H. G. Liddell and R. Scott, rev. by H. S. Jones (Oxford 1925–36)

LTK   Lexikon für Theologie und Kirche (Freiburg i. Br. 1930–38)

OCD   Oxford Classical Dictionary (Oxford 1949)

PG   J. P. Migne, Patrologia graeca (Paris 1857–66)

PL   J. P. Migne, Patrologia latina (Paris 1844–55)

PO   Patrologia orientalis (Paris 1903–)

RAC   Reallexikon für Antike und Christentum (Stuttgart 1950–)

RE   A. Pauly, G. Wissowa, W. Kroll, etc., Real-Encyclopädie der classischen Altertumswissenschaft (Stuttgart 1893–)

Roscher   W. H. Roscher, Lexikon der griechischen und römischen Mythologie (Leipzig 1884–1937)

INTRODUCTION

[1] PG 6.182: cf. H. Dodwell, *Dissertationes in Irenaeum* (Oxford 1689) 488.

[2] Eusebius, *Hist. eccl.* 6.6, 5.10, and 6.14.8, where the letter of Alexander of Jerusalem is quoted.

[3] 'Ephesus, Athens and Alexandria,' *Thought* 13 (1938) 107.

[4] Cod. Parisin. 451, written in A.D. 914 by Baanes for Arethas.

[5] *Strom.* 1.1.14. For R. B. Tollinton's comments, see *Clement of Alexandria. A Study in Christian Liberalism* (London 1914) 1.12.

[6] *Strom.* 1.7.37.6.

[7] *Bibliotheca* cod. 155.

[8] The name of Athenagoras is mentioned in *De res.* 37.1, where a substantial passage has been borrowed from him. The same passage is quoted by Epiphanius, *Haer.* 64.21, and by Photius, *Bibl.* cod. 234.

[9] Tatian, *Orat.* 6, sketches the topic briefly.

[10] Cf. *Digest* 50.4.1.2 and 50.4.18.11.

[11] PG 6.188–97.

[12] Cf. Epiphanius, *Haer.* 48.4; Hippolytus, *De antichr.* 2; Justin, *Dial.* 115; Ps.-Justin, *Cohort.* 8; Tertullian, *Adv. Marc.* 4.22; Philo, *Quis rer. div. haer.* 264; Plato, *Phaedr.* 249d.

[13] In *Embassy* 33. See nn. 288 and 291 on that passage.

[14] 'Ante-Nicene Interpretations of the Sayings on Divorce,' JTS 20 (1919) 232 ff.

[15] *Mand.* 4.4.1.

[16] Cf. A. Harnack, *Geschichte der altchristlichen Literatur: Die Chronologie* 1 (Leipzig 1897) 317 f.

[17] *Oxy. Pap.* 485, line 39. This is an Egyptian document dated A.D. 178. For the style of Commodus as Armenian victor after 180, see *Oxy. Pap.* 513, line 50, from A.D. 184.

[18] See further RE II A 16, line 47 s.v. 'Sarmaticus.'

[19] Tertullian, *De an.* 23: *omnium haereticorum condimentarium.*

[20] *Rep.* 388c, *Gorg.* 524a, *Phaed.* 104b, *Phaedr.* 244b and 246e, *Tim.* 28c and 40e, *Pol.* 269d, *Epist.* 2.312e.

[21] Justin, 1 *Apol.* 60.7: Clement, *Strom.* 5.14.103.1–4.

[22] *Emb.* 10. ἀνεκδιηγήτῳ comes from 2 Cor. 9.15 and is not Platonic.

[23] *Emb.* 15.

[24] *Res.* 12.

[25] *Emb.* 24. The term ἀποχεόμενον is used in *Emb.* 23. Plato (*Rep.* 509b) makes goodness prior to being.

[26] Clement, *Strom.* 4.25.

[27] *Epist.* 65.7 Lodge's translation is cited.

[28] *Tim.* 48a.

[29] *Emb.* 24.

[30] See *Res.* n. 70.

[31] *Laws* 899d.

[32] *Tim.* 28c.

[33] In *Emb.* 12 the terms ἕνωσις and κοινωνία are used to describe the relation of Father to Son. The expression used in *Emb.* 10, that the Father is in the Son ἐνότητι κὰι δυνάμει Πνεύματος, 'by the powerful union of the Spirit,' has sometimes been taken to mean that Father and Son are one by the oneness of their godhead, Πνεῦμα being taken to mean godhead rather than Spirit. Maran started the vogue for this latter interpretation and it has been adopted by many later scholars. As far as one can judge from Athenagoras's use of the word in the *Embassy*, it always means, when applied to God, the Holy Spirit. There are sixteen places in the *Embassy* where it can have only this meaning; two more are possibly to be translated either as 'Spirit' or as 'godhead,' and there is this place. The probabilities are therefore entirely in favour of the translation 'Spirit' here.

[34] If the Father and the Word are one, it is hard to see that the Father can be conceived as existing prior to the Word. Athenagoras expressly denies (*Emb.* 10) that the Word is created, thus giving in advance the lie to those who would make him an Arian in disguise.

[35] The term ἀπόρροια, or outflow, is applied to the Spirit in *Emb.* 10 and 24. This cannot imply subordination of the Spirit to the other two Persons, for the three are joined several times (*Emb.* 10, 12, and 24) in expressions where no distinction of rank between the three is made. 'That two Divine Persons and an impersonal emanation should be thus enumerated together, by so philosophic a writer as Athenagoras, is not conceivable.' This verdict by H. L. Mansel (DCB 1.206) must surely be accepted.

[36] See *Emb.* n. 145.

[37] See Melito, *Hom.* 82f. (Bonner), and *Apost. Const.* 8.12.6–27.

[38] Apollonius, the martyr of A.D. 185, when asked to sacrifice, says: 'As to sacrifices, I and all Christians offer a bloodless sacrifice to God, Lord of heaven and earth and of the sea and of every living being, in behalf of the spiritual and rational images who have been appointed by the Providence of God to rule over the earth' (*Acts* 8; trans. from

the Armenian by F. C. Conybeare, *The Armenian Apology and Acts of Apollonius and other Monuments of Early Christianity* [London 1894]). This can hardly escape being taken as a reference to the Eucharist. The use of the phrase in *Testamentum Levi* 3.6 may be due to a Christian editor, as the words are not found in all the MSS.

[39] See *Emb.* 32 and n. 283.

[40] The hymn is published in *Oxy. Pap.* 1786, along with the music that it was sung to, and again in PO 18.507. The papyrus has a 3rd-century mercantile account on the reverse side. The hymn must therefore have been in use in Egypt soon after the time of Athenagoras.

TEXT

EMBASSY FOR THE CHRISTIANS

¹ Rome did not impose her own system of law upon the provincial peoples of her empire in their dealings with one another. Disputes between *cives* and provincial *socii* had, however, usually to be settled by Roman law. Gallio (Acts 18.15) was acting with full Roman legality in refusing to be drawn into a dispute among Jews about their religion. The general Roman attitude towards the religions of the provinces was one of disdain. Juvenal (*Sat.* 15) expresses this attitude in his ridicule of Egyptian worship.

² Geffcken (162) calls Athenagoras half-educated because he puts into his argument the words τὰ πάτρια here, as if in 176 only pagans, and not Christians, could appeal to *ancestral* worship and as if it was exposing the whole Christian case to jeopardy by introducing the idea of their worship being in peaceful possession. It is true that Tertullian and others can boast of the newness of Christianity in their time, in contrast with the effete and dying paganism around them, but by this time there would be many places where Christians could claim more than a century of practice. Some of the Oriental cults, on the other hand, could not claim as much. Christians like the contemporary bishop of Ephesus, Polycrates, could claim that they had a long line of ancestors who had been Christian (cf. Eusebius, *Hist. eccl.* 5.24.6).

³ Hector, son of Priam and Hecuba, was honoured by sacrifices at Troy, as Lucian (*Deor. conc.* 12) attests. Lucian jestingly makes the gods complain of such usurpation of divine honours, in a passage somewhat similar to Athenagoras's list.

⁴ Helen, wife of Menelaus and cause of the Trojan war, was worshipped at Sparta along with her husband (Pausanias 3.15.3 and 3.19.9). Isocrates (*Laud. Hel.* 63) makes it clear that she received worship as a goddess and not merely as one of heroic status, but there is no evidence for her identification with Nemesis-Adrasteia, the goddess of Necessity. It is to be remarked, however, that Athenaeus (p. 334, citing the *Cypria*) and Philodemus (*De pietate*) make her the daughter of Nemesis, and that Nemesis under the title of Adrasteia was worshipped at the place named Adrasteia (cf. Stephanus Byz. s.v.) in the area of Troy.

9   123

5 Zeus had many titles in Sparta. The ancient evidence for Agamem-
nonios as one of them is found in Staphylus of Naucratis (FHG 4.506
fr. 10; cf. Clement, *Protr.* 2.38.2). A long study by J. Harris in *Archiv
für Religionswissenschaft* 23 (1925) 359ff. denies that this evidence has
any value, but we are hardly in a position to know for certain. The
excavations at Sparta have shown a cult of Helen and Menelaus as
gods going back to 1000 B.C. It would be risky to say that Agamemnon, brother of Menelaus in the saga, did not share this cult. For the
excavations, see *Annual of the British School at Athens* 15 (1908–09)
108ff.

6 Phylonoe, daughter of Leda and Tyndareus, was made immortal
by Artemis (Apollodorus 3.10.6). There is no archaeological evidence
for her cult at Sparta, but the Dioscuri, who were worshipped there,
are called Tyndaridai on local inscriptions (IG 5.1.305, etc.).

7 Enodia was a cult title for Artemis. There is evidence of its use
at Epidaurus (IG 4.1191 f.) and elsewhere. No such evidence has been
found in Sparta itself, but the Spartan dependency of Thera has supplied some: cf. *Mitteilungen d. deutschen archäologischen Instituts, Athen.
Abt.* 25 (1900) 462. The title implied guardianship of roads or tracks.
Perhaps Phylonoe was accepted at Sparta as the secondary guardian
of these.

8 Erectheus is the cult companion of Poseidon at Athens (IG 3.276
and Pausanias 1.26.5; also Herodotus 8.55). The combined title Erec-
theus-Poseidon occurs on inscriptions (I.G 3.276) and in the *Vitae
decem oratorum* (845B) ascribed to Plutarch.

9 Pandrosos, Aglauros, and Herse were daughters of Cecrops.
The Plynteria were held in honour of Aglauros; Plutarch (*Alcib.*
34) speaks of the secret rites that accompanied the removal of the
peplos from the statue of Athena Polias six days before the end
of Thargelion each year. There was also a δειπνοφορία in honour
of the three sisters (cf. RE 1.828 f.). The scholiast on Aristophanes
(*Lys.* 439) claims Pandrosos as a byname of Athena, but originally
they were distinct personalities, as Philochorus (cited by Harpocration
s.v. ἐπίβοιον) shows. Aglauros is the name of the second sister on all
inscriptions, but by an easy letter change, this name was assimilated
to the common adjective Agraulos, meaning 'countrified.' In the
legend the sisters are given charge by Athena of a box containing
Erichthonius, the infant guarded by two serpents. One of the sisters
opens the box, whereupon the serpents come out and pursue the girls,
who go mad and leap into the sea (Hyginus, *Fab.* 166). The accuracy
of Athenagoras on these points is defended in RE 18b.555.

10 There is a verbal reminiscence here of the Dionysia Κατ' ἀγρούς

or Κατὰ δήμους. This was the lesser Dionysia, held in the month Poseidon, in contrast with the greater or City Dionysia.

11 Ridicule of Egyptian animal-worship was a commonplace of philosophers of religion. See Cicero (*De nat. deor.* 3.15.39), Lucian (*Iupp. trag.* 42), Aristides (*Apol.* 12.6–9), Clement (*Protr.* 2.41.4, *Paed.* 3.2.4.3 f., etc.), and the Apologists generally. The best description of the worship is probably that of Herodotus (2.65–69).

12 The words from 'to us' down to the end of the sentence are re- jected by Schwartz as a clumsy addition to the text, introducing a mention of the Christians before the emperor's mind has been pre- pared to hear about them. Geffcken, Goodspeed, Ubaldi, and Bardy have followed Schwartz, but it does not seem necessary to agree with them. It would not be unskilful, but on the contrary adroit, for Athen- agoras to mention those he represents and to keep the emperor in suspense for a moment before he spoke the word that identified them 'Christians.'

13 The verb ἀπεχθάνεται is a true passive and is impersonal.

14 The relevance of these remarks about profound peace to the dating of the work is discussed in the Introd. p. 10 f.

15 The attack upon the name (*nomen ipsum*) was distinguished by the Christian apologists, following Pliny's letter (*Epist. ad Trai.* 96) and before him St. Peter (1 Peter 4.15 f.), from the crimes against the natural law (*flagitia cohaerentia nomini*) which were ascribed to them.

16 The patience of the Christians is described in terms that recall Matt. 5.39 f. without explicit quotation. The duty of not going to law is derived from 1 Cor. 6.2.

17 The freedom of the Christians from the crimes imputed to them was a common ground to all the Apologists (cf. Tertullian, *Apol.* 45, or Minucius Felix 35.6). Justin (1 *Apol.* 29) tells of one Christian in Egypt who volunteered to be castrated by the prefect of Egypt to show that the charge of promiscuity in Christian assemblies was false.

18 Geffcken's correction of the genitive εὐεργεσίας for the dative has been accepted for the translation. Later Greek usage tended to obscure the distinction between genitive and dative constructions with the verb κοινωνέω, but Athenagoras himself is not likely to have been so careless, whatever the scribes of his work may have done later on.

19 'What's in a name?' is a common sentiment to-day, but in an age when magic held such large sway, this was by no means so obvious. The magical papyri have brought that home to us.

20 For the characterization of Christianity as a school of philosophy,

see an article, 'Ephesus, Athens, and Alexandria,' by the present writer in *Thought* 13 (1938) 101–103. The rescript obtained by the Epicureans at Athens from Hadrian on the occasion of his visit in 121 (cf. *Archiv f. Gesch. d. Philosophie* 4 [1890] 486–91) was a precedent that any Christian must have hoped to see extended to his own creed.

21 With the end of this section Athenagoras has finished his introduction and has done his rhetorical best to capture the sympathetic hearing of the emperors. Now he will make the enumeration of the heads of his discourse, listing the charges to which he must reply.

22 The charges are the usual ones (found e.g. in Justin, 1 *Apol.* 26.7, Minucius Felix 28, Tertullian, *Apol.* 7.1, and the *Letter of the Church of Lyons and Vienne*: Eusebius, *Hist. eccl.* 5.1.14). Thyestes was tricked by his enemy (and brother or father) Atreus into eating the flesh of his own children. Oedipus, whom the psychologists have appropriated in modern times, was similarly beguiled into committing incest with his mother Iocasta: see OCD 618. Pliny's remarks about Christian food being harmless (*Epist. ad Trai.* 96.7) show that he had heard of the charge of cannibalistic meals.

23 The derivation of the law of nature from what animals did by instinct was a Stoic idea. Panaetius among the Stoics gave wider scope to the animal side of man's nature, refusing to regard man as a more or less disembodied intellect (Cicero, *De off.* 1.28.101, *Tusc. disp.* 2.20.47). Cicero was largely Panaetius's disciple. Earlier still, Aristotle (in *Hist. anim.* 630 b 31 and 631 a 1–5) tells of a repugnance to 'incest' observed among camels and horses, though such incest was encouraged by horse breeders (*ibid.* 576 a 17–20). His story of the horse that killed itself after being tricked into such a union was believed and used by St. Thomas.

24 The principle of strife in all nature was canonized by Empedocles. According to him the world began in love and harmony, but gradually strife, the disruptive force in the world, broke in upon the primitive harmony and waged constant war against it (cf. Aristotle, *De caelo* 301 a 15).

25 The MS reading is κελεύοντες μὴ ὁμονοεῖν. As this hardly yields any sense here, the emperors not being likely to have forbidden concord, emendation has been tried. Schwartz proposed μὴ ὁμολογεῖν, with the sense that the Christians were told to deny their faith, but it is not possible to believe that Athenagoras, had he wanted to express that idea, should have wrapped it up in a negative: 'bidding us not to confess.' Lindner took the same emendation to mean that they were forbidden to plead guilty, but no trace of such an imperial edict exists, nor can its influence be seen in later statements of Roman

law. An emendation much nearer the text is the old one of Dom
Maran, who suggested μὴ μηνύειν. By haplography this would
become μηνύειν, which, not being intelligible to a scribe, would then
be lengthened into μὴ ὁμονοεῖν at some date before A.D. 914. The
sense then becomes: 'not to lay informations,' and the evidence for
such an imperial edict can be found in what Trajan wrote in reply to
Pliny: 'Informations offered anonymously should have no place in
any criminal trial. It is a pernicious precedent and not in keeping with
the spirit of our times' (Pliny, *Epist. ad Trai.*: 97.2). This emendation
has been adopted for the translation. Geffcken at this point rewrites the
Greek on a large scale, and Bardy translates what is not there at all.
Richardson translates: 'It is only the confession of a name that you
forbid,' thus accepting the emendation of Schwartz, but it would be
ludicrous to suppose that the emperors had proscribed the Name and
had said nothing about the *flagitia cohaerentia nomini*.

26 This is a statement rather than a request. In listening to the
Christian apologia the emperors will be doing no more to favour them
than by listening to stories of Thyestean banquets they favour the
enemies of Christianity.

27 Diagoras of Melos, a lyric poet, satirized in Aristophanes's *Clouds*
and *Frogs* (423 and 414 B.C.) and the stock example of atheism throughout antiquity, is said to have lost his belief in the gods when one who
had sworn a false oath by them went unpunished (*Schol. in Nubes*
830). The Athenians (*Birds* 1073 and *Schol. ad loc.*) went so far as to
condemn him to death for mocking their mysteries. No writings of
his survive save a few broken lines of verse. He may have died a natural
death (so Suidas), but there was a story (Athenaeus, *Deip.* 611a) that
he was drowned at sea in his flight from Athens.

28 The argument from design has already a long history before it is
taken up by Athenagoras here. Socrates discovered it for himself, as
Plato makes him say in the *Phaedo* (97b), whether there were other
Greek philosophers who used it before him or not. It was favoured by
the Stoics, and was much exploited in the 2nd century A.D. Galen
argued from the fact that eyelashes do not grow, while eyebrows do,
that the human body was wisely adapted to the purpose of living by a
creator. Marcus Aurelius (in his *Meditations* 12.28) puts the argument
to himself. The argument did not, of course, prompt a Stoic, who was
attached to the idea of an indwelling deity, to entertain any idea of
God's transcendence, and so Stoic and Christian held the argument
in different terms. It is used by Tertullian (*Apol.* 17), Minucius Felix
(17), and others.

29 *Not subject to becoming* is a rendering of ἀγένητον. The MS reads

unbegotten, ἀγέννητον. In the contrasted clause γενητήν is used in the MS, not γεννητήν. An exact parallel to this confusion occurs in Plato (*Tim.* 52a) where the same two apparently unsymmetrical adjectives are used. Athenagoras, being a Platonist, is probably influenced by Plato towards a certain carelessness or indifference in not making a sharp distinction between the two words. See G. L. Prestige's discussion of the two words in JTS 24 (1922–23) 486–96 as also in his *God in Patristic Thought* (London 1952) 40; also a note by J. Lebreton in his *Histoire du dogme de la Trinité* (Paris 1927) 2.635–47.

30 Creation by the Word is taught by St. John (1.3) and St. Paul (Col. 1.15 f.).

31 The fragment of Euripides (=Nauck fr. 900) is not found elsewhere. The first line lacks one foot to complete the metre. This has been variously supplied. If it was the same man who had previously been made happy by Zeus and was now afflicted, this would be a lesson in the mistrust of Providence.

32 The fragment (=Nauck fr. 941) is cited by Heraclitus, by Cicero (*De nat. deor.* 2.25.65) and by Lucian (*Iupp. trag.* 41). Lucian (*ibid.*) has also the next fragment (=Nauck fr. 480), and my rendering of both is taken from H. W. and F. G. Fowler's translation of L. (3.100). It is probable that he and Athenagoras have been using some philosophical manual where the texts occurred together. Cicero turns the first fragment into a confession that the ether is God, but this is not a fair rendering of the Greek.

33 The text has three words, ἀέρα ἀιθέρος γῆς, which have no exact relation to the rest of the sentence. By altering the first of these to ἀέρος, Fabricius made them all genitives and brought them into the construction. His emendation has been accepted for the translation.

34 This quotation from Sophocles (=Nauck fr. 1025) appears in a number of Christian apologists (twice in Clement of Alexandria: *Protr.* 7.74.2 and *Strom.* 5.14.113.2; in Ps.-Justin, *Cohort.* 18 and *De monarch.* 2; in Theodoret, *Graec. aff. cur.* 7.46; and in Cyril of Alexandria, *Adv. Iul.* 1. p. 32a). Clement quotes nine lines of the fragment and gives out that it was cited by Hecataeus in a work on *Abraham and the Egyptians*. This work, used by Josephus also (*Ant.* 1.158), is probably a forgery which masqueraded under the name of Hecataeus of Abdera, a Greek philosopher of the 3rd century B.C. The fragment of verse is hardly by Sophocles. It reads too much like the first article of the Creed and may be the work of a Hellenized Jew. Its language belongs to the diction of the tragedians, but Sophocles was too much of a believer in the old gods to have produced it. The teaching of the fragment as it is given by Clement is that mortals mistake the

flash of the waves and the majesty of the wind for deities and waste their piety on gold and ivory statues. Thus the poet could be said to point out wherein was the true beauty of the heavens and the earth, in their reflecting the beauty of God. There is hence no need to change the MS reading here.

35 Philolaus, a Pythagorean philosopher, from Croton (modern Cotrone) in S. Italy, was a contemporary of Socrates. A few fragments said to have been taken from his works survive, but their authenticity is doubtful.

36 Lysis (cf. Plutarch, *De gen. Soc.* 575e) was a well-known Pythagorean of Tarentum. The attempt of some German critics to interpret his ἄρρητος ἀριθμός as an irrational number or surd fails owing to the fact that these surds were discovered after his time.

37 Opsimus (the restoration of the name from ὄψει of the MS seems certain) is only once mentioned elsewhere, by Iamblichus (*Vit. Pyth.* 36).

38 The tetractys was a Pythagorean discovery, namely that by setting out units in a pattern to represent the sum of the first four numbers, one reached the perfect number, ten:

St. Augustine was thrilled, in his day, to find that if one carried on the process up to seventeen (the sum of the ten commandments and the seven gifts of the Holy Ghost), one had the number of the fish caught in the miraculous draught—153: cf. *Serm.* 249.3 (PL 38.1162 f.); also 250.3 and 251.4.5. See M. Pontet, *L'exégèse de S. Augustin prédicateur* (Paris 1944) 512.

38a The Doxographers (literally, writers of opinions) were philosophers of second rank who after the time of Aristotle made collections of the opinions of their betters. The chief of them was Aetius, who lived about fifty years before Athenagoras. For their works, see H. Diels, *Doxographi graeci* (Berlin 1879). Though very pedestrian, they are the first historians of philosophy.

39 The first extract from Plato (*Tim.* 28c) had a great success with the Christian apologists, as it seemed to foreshadow the idea of Revelation. See Justin, 2 *Apol.* 10.6; Minucius Felix 19; Tertullian, *Apol.* 46.9; etc.

40 This extract from Plato (*Tim.* 41a) has one notable corruption of

wording as it stands here in the MS, reading ἀδύνατα for ἃ ἄλυτα. This goes to show how easily changes from the strange to the more familiar may have been made in other parts of the MS, where an outside check is impossible.

⁴¹ The word 'cherishing' translates κρατοῦντες of the MS, whereas Schwartz and others have changed the MS into κρατύνοντες which would have to be rendered: 'confirming that he is God.'

⁴² Aristotle may be quoted here, but it is generally thought more likely that a manual has been used such as the *Placita* of Aëtius (the Ps.-Plutarch). But as there is no exact verbal correspondence between Aëtius and Athenagoras, the latter may have used some other source book of Aristotelian philosophy now lost. The *Placita* credit Aristotle with holding that God is in charge of the sphere of the whole (the outermost sphere), while Athenagoras thinks that Aristotle meant this sphere to be the body of God. This misconception of Aristotle's doctrine may be Jewish, coming from Philo or a disciple, but one cannot be certain.

⁴³ The derivation of the name Zeus from ζέω and of Hera from ἀέρα is Stoic (cf. Cicero, *De nat. deor.* 2.25.65 f.).

⁴⁴ After the words, 'they can speak and write,' the MS has almost the whole of section 13 inserted in error, a scribe having omitted one or two leaves of the quire he was copying, and then, when he had found the missing leaves and copied them, not cancelling the superfluous passage.

⁴⁵ The law against the Christians is the subject of much dispute. For a modern statement of the argument, see J. Lebreton–J. Zeiller in Fliche-Martin, *Histoire de l'Église* I (Paris 1946) 292 ff.; in the same sense, N. H. Baynes, CAH 12 (1939) 654. H. Grégoire (*Anal. Boll.* 69 [1951] 1–30), in an ill-considered attempt to postdate the beginning of the martyrdoms, entirely neglects the question of the law. The article, 'Christenverfolgung,' in RAC 2 (1954) 1159–1228, by J. Vogt and H. Last, denies there was any specific law; while that by A. Amore in EC 9 (1952) 1198–1202, 'Persecuzioni contro i Cristiani,' says that there was.

⁴⁶ The theory of συμπάθεια here appealed to may be found in Plutarch (*De def. orac.* 438a), where it is used to explain how the felicitous conjunction of the vapours of the Delphic cavern with a woman of the right temperament (the Pythia) produced the oracles naturally. Others might try the vapours without result, and the woman, if consulted elsewhere, would be unable to reply. Here it is applied by Athenagoras to the workings of grace preparing a way for the revelation of Christ. His words have not the precision of the Scholastic

theory of connatural knowledge, for he is talking as Paul did to the Areopagus.

[47] There is no longer any feeling among Christians like Athenagoras that the prophets were Jewish and therefore alien. All their utterances were deemed to have some reference to Christ and His Church (which is the true Israel), and therefore Athenagoras does not pause to explain that 'our prophets' were really Jewish.

[48] The theory of Inspiration is further outlined in section 9. Philo, *Quis rer. div. her.* 259, has similar language. Perhaps I may refer to what I have written on the subject in the *Catholic Commentary on Holy Scripture* (London 1953) 35e.

[49] The proof of the uniqueness of God that is here given is by *reductio ad absurda*. Suppose the contrary, that God is two or more: then these two beings either are generically related or they are not. If they are, they must either be equal instances of godhead or unequal. If equal, they would be parallel specimens of one genus. But that is absurd, for all specimens are generic by relation to an origin or model. But there could be no model for the gods—ergo. If however they are unequal, they will be complementary (like the limbs of a body); but complementarity implies divisibility, and hence a liability to corruption, which is absurd in a god. If now they are not generically related but disparate, either they are each eternally self-existent or not. If so, then one of them is lord of this universe. Where, then, does the other have his universe? Nowhere, unless absurdities are to be allowed. If again, one of them is not self-existent but comes to be, absurdities would again be the result.

[50] As Geffcken has already argued (179 n. 1), the various omissions from the text contrived here by Schwartz and Wilamowitz do not seem required. On the other hand, Gesner's correction of οὐδὲν εἰ μὴ προνοῇ πεποίηκεν into οὐδὲ προνοεῖ εἰ μὴ πεποίηκεν does improve the argument and has been adopted.

[51] The argument about God's location was a stock subject of debate in Stoic schools of philosophy: cf. Cicero, *De nat. deor.* 1.37.103; Philo, *De conf. ling.* 138; Justin, *Dial.* 127.2. The comparison of the unity of reasonable beings with that of the human body is approved in Marcus Aurelius, *Med.* 7.13 and 8.34 f. The rest of the material for this argument and its closely-knit logical structure belong to Athenagoras himself.

[52] ἀμυήτους was Geffcken's correction of the text, which has ἀνοήτους. The correction was not needed, for ἀνοήτους can be used in an active sense to mean 'without understanding,' with a genitive dependent upon it (cf. LSJ s.v. IIb).

⁵³ The theory of Inspiration is to some extent indebted to Philo, who (*Quod Deus sit immut.* 24) compares the soul to a lyre whose strings God attunes, so that the owner of it can lead a virtuous life. This, coupled with Philo's idea that the prophets were held by a divine enthusiasm, like Bacchanals, led to the idea of God striking the lyre of the prophet's soul and producing what He willed. Athenagoras has the Philonic terms ἔνθεον πνεῦμα and ἔκστασις λογισμοῦ here (cf. *De spec. leg.* 49 and *De decal.* 35 and 175), but the image of the flute and flute-player seems to be independent of Philo. Original too is the idea of God working *with* (as well as *through*) the prophet, an idea suggested by Athenagoras's terms συγχρησαμένου and ἃ ἐνηργοῦντο, (cf. I Cor. 12.6). Theophilus, *Ad Autol.* 2.9, Clement of Alexandria, *Strom.* 6.18.168, Ps.-Justin, *Cohort.* 8.4, copy this idea of Athenagoras.

⁵⁴ The Old Testament quotations come from Exod. 20.2 f., Isa. 44.6, 43.10 f., and 66.1.

⁵⁵ Athenagoras well shows how the attributes of God are established by what was later to be called the *via remotionis et eminentiae*, or the way of negation and extrapolation. He lists the negative attributes first, and then those wherein God excels the positive perfections of human nature, ending up with God's unique creative activity.

⁵⁶ The real danger for an apologist was that the pagan would be only too ready to accept the idea of God having a son, with his memories of the son Zeus had by Alcmene or by others. The laughter would be caused by surprise at thinking to find that, after all this plea for monotheism, the Christian was just like himself in his beliefs. See also Theophilus, *Ad Autol.* 2.22.

⁵⁷ Philo does not appear to have used the terms ἰδέα καὶ ἐνέργεια for the Logos. Indeed he generally has ἐνέργεια in the plural. Athenagoras's originality here makes one chary of accepting facile identifications of his theology with that of Philo, who yet has anticipated him in using the comparison of the Spirit of God to the radiance sent forth from the sun—cf. *De opif. mund.* 146; *De mon.* 38–40—a comparison that reappears in Tertullian, *Apol.* 21.12.

⁵⁸ The words are from John 1.3, though their order is changed. When Athenagoras adds that all things were made 'after His fashion' πρὸς αὐτοῦ or 'agreeably to Him,' he is stating what is implied in Col. 1.16 f., though it is only in the Scotist theology of the Incarnation that the idea receives full justice.

⁵⁹ The idea of considering the Spirit as the uniting power of the Father and the Son is here set forth for the first time in Christian theology. No doubt one can derive it from certain Johannine phrases, but Athenagoras has supplied it with its first technical terms. The

absence of the article with πνεῦμα is, I think, a reminiscence of a similar vagueness in some New Testament texts, and possibly also due to a prudent desire not to be too explicit here about the central mystery of Christianity.

⁶⁰ The Pauline πρωτότοκος is not used, but a more philosophical paraphrase, πρῶτον γέννημα. Justin uses πρωτότοκος some twelve times of Christ, has this term once in 1 *Apol.* 21.1 and γέννημα alone at *Dial.* 62.4 and 129.4. Philo, *De post. Caini* 63, had used it of human offspring.

⁶¹ What Athenagoras wants to say is obviously that the Son is eternal although begotten and hence pre-existent to all creation, and that He is in fact the one who organized the material creation from an undifferentiated state into a world of order, weight, and measure. But his text is corrupt at a vital point. We do not know exactly to what he compared the undifferentiated material of the world. A possibility might be ἡσυχαίας instead of the unintelligible γῆς οχίας of the MS. This conjecture has been translated in this version.

⁶² The text, from Prov. 8.22 (Sept.—tr. by Brenton), became the starting point of Arius's heresy (cf. Agapius, PO 7.544). Athenagoras is not yet open to these ideas, though A. Puech, *Les apologistes grecs du 2ᵉ siècle de notre ère* (Paris 1912) 188 f., wishes, on account of the use of λογικός here, to interpret him as saying that the Word is a faculty rather than a person prior to His generation, which would then be considered to have taken place at the moment of creation. Newman already in his *Arians* (London 1871) 97 f. and 204 had rejected, and with reason, this interpretation of Athenagoras. The epithet λογικός is not applied to the Father by any other apologist (though Tatian, *Orat.* 5.1, speaks of God having a λογικὴ δύναμις). Hence it seems fair to translate it in the way adopted here, as being a first-time use of the adjective in a somewhat tentative association with the term *Father*. Richardson has no justification for translating τάξις here as rank instead of the correct word *order* and so making Athenagoras reduce the Spirit to a lower level than the Father and the Son. Elsewhere in the work τάξις undoubtedly means order rather than rank.

⁶³ The description of the Spirit as an outflow may have been influenced by Philo, *De gig.* 25-27, who uses the image of a fire that is not diminished by the torches lit from it, and that of a well whose waters grow ever sweeter by being continually drawn, to illustrate the idea of God remaining infinite in spite of emanations proceeding from Him. Still he does not seem to have used the word ἀπόρροια in this connexion (see Leisegang's *Index verborum* s.v., where the only example, *De spec. leg.* 1.40, is of the word being used in its literal sense of an outflow

of light from the sun). There is no trace of this exact image in the Apostolic Fathers or in the earlier Apologists. Tertullian has it in full, *Apol.* 21, and elaborates it in *Adv. Prax.* 8 (cf. the remarks to same in E. Evans's edition [London 1948] 239 f.). Justin indeed has the Philonic comparison of the fire and the torch (*Dial.* 61.2 and 128.4) and speaks *ibid.* 128.3 of the Logos coming from the Father like the ray coming down from the sun while remaining indivisibly united to its source and departing again at sunset. This idea he may have elaborated from Philo and Heb. 1.3. The originality of Athenagoras lies in his applying this image to the Spirit and in finding a distinctive word for it.

64 Heb. 1.14 and Apoc. 22.9 are sufficient warrant for Athenagoras calling the angels ministers. Philo, *De human.* 74, calls them ministers, too, but this need not mean that Athenagoras has copied him. Justin, 2 *Apol.* 5.2, sets forth the doctrine that to the angels has been entrusted the care of men and of all things sublunary. The mention of angels immediately after the Trinity here shows that they were considered to belong to the θεολογία, whereas all that concerned the Incarnation and God's plan of salvation belonged to the οἰκονομία or *dispensation.* An embarrassing passage of Justin (1 *Apol.* 6.2), where angels are named before the Holy Spirit, is cleared up by this clear statement of Athenagoras.

65 Taken from Matt. 5.44 f., with an addition from Luke 6.28. The Sermon on the Mount was particularly suited to show the nobility and reasonableness of Christianity. Cf. also Clement, *Strom.* 4.14.95.2, and Eusebius, *Praep. ev.* 13.7.5., where the same conflation of texts occurs.

66 The 'three mysteries of a shout' which were in the silence of God, according to Ignatius, *Eph.* 19.1 (cf. ASW 1.67 and n. 46), afford a precedent for taking Athenagoras to be playing here upon the word *Logos.* God's message to men broke forth in a world that was hopeless and by comparison silent. Hence the good news is like a shout that breaks a painful silence of suspense. I do not think that Athenagoras is merely complaining or feigning to complain of being interrupted by hostile shouting in his presence, as Bardy and Richardson suppose. If that were so, he ought to say that his discourse had become audible *in spite of* many shouts. No one can suppose that what he has just said has been the most provocative part of his whole speech.

67 The metaphor in ἀνάγειν may be that of launching out, but more probably, as in Plato, *Rep.* 528a, it is that of falling back upon a stronghold when attacked.

68 The masters who taught analysis of syllogisms might be any of the philosophers of the age. Geffcken refers to Chrysippus (*Stoic.*

vet. fr. II pp. 5–7, 45–47, 59 and 125). It was a rhetorical commonplace to denounce logic-chopping as unprofitable. Seneca excelled in this (*Ep.* 45.6–10) and Tertullian (*De praescr. haer.* 7) has a famous attack on Aristotle. M. Aurelius himself (*Med.* 1.17.9) thanked the gods that although he loved philosophy, he had not fallen into the grip of a sophist who might have led him to spend his life on the analysis of syllogisms or vain speculation about problems in the clouds. Hence Athenagoras may have scored a hit with his remarks. R. Walzer in his *Galen on Jews and Christians* (Oxford 1949) 75–86, has put forward the idea that Galen influenced a group of Christians at Rome headed by Theodotus of Byzantium to take an interest in logic and to apply it to their theological beliefs to the annoyance of 'the somewhat authoritarian bishop of Rome, Victor.' If the attack on logical excesses had begun ten years before the days of Pope Victor, it is hard to see any great novelty in what either Theodotus or Pope Victor did.

69 The participle σαφηνιζόντων is to be understood with the string of objects τὰ ὁμώνυμα etc. Then there is no need to suppose a lacuna with Schwartz and Geffcken. Rather the verb εἰσί should be omitted, as the scribe of the secondary MS a seems to have understood.

70 M. Aurelius (*Med.* 7.22) bases love of enemies on a fellow feeling for all other men who are one's kindred, ignorant like oneself and in a brief space destined to die like oneself. He adds as the main point for a Stoic that one's enemy cannot do harm to the deity or governing principle of the universe present in oneself both before and after the bodily injury. The idea that a man should love his murderer does not follow very easily from such a line of thought.

71 There is a crux here, but it can be confined to the word ἑαυτούς for which some editors read ἐπ' αὐτούς, a reading adopted in the translation. The participle μεταλλεύοντες has probably been used for μεταλλάσσοντες, as in Wisd. 4.12 (Sept.), where a similar confusion of the two verbs occurs. Plato has used μεταλλάσσειν in *Tim.* 19a with the meaning 'to substitute' or 'to put something in the place of something else.' This sense has been adopted in the translation here. Bardy with: 'Ces hommes ne cessent de creuser leurs mystères avec de mauvaises dispositions,' and Richardson: 'They ever persist in delving into the evil mysteries of their sophistry,' both make philosophy into a black art, which can hardly have been Athenagoras's intent. Geffcken keeps μεταλλεύω in its proper sense and supposes that it can take two objects.

72 From 1 Cor. 1.26 the idea that Christians included 'not many wise, not many powerful' was familiar. Justin, 1 *Apol.* 60.11, echoed

it. Tatian, *Orat.* 32.1, boasted of it. Origen, *C. Cels.* 3.44 and 6.14, was troubled by it. By his time it had become a jibe used by anti-Christian propaganda. Pope Callistus had been a slave and Hippolytus among others looked down on him for it. Cf. A. Harnack, *Die Mission und Ausbreitung des Christentums* (4. ed. Leipzig 1924) 559 ff.

73 There is an opposition of intellect and will, and a contrast between benefit to self and to others. Simple folk may have strong wills but weak heads. Faith does not help their minds much, but, influencing their conduct once they have freely assented, it benefits others greatly. Thus early is emphasis given to the freedom of the act of faith.

74 The closing words are reminiscent of Matt. 5.39, 40, and 42.

75 Verbs of taking away should have accusatives. One cannot be sure that Athenagoras would not have used a genitive of the thing (deprive us *of* our souls), and therefore it is not wise to correct the syntax as Schwartz and Geffcken do.

76 The correlative of τηλικοῦτον is ὅσον. It may be that Athenagoras wrote the latter word and that abbreviation in the MS has destroyed further trace of it, leaving only ὧν. The genitives can then depend on this word ὅσον, and the sense, though somewhat strange, does not need the addition of μισθόν, as suggested by Wilamowitz. To add such a word is to rewrite the text according to one's own fancy. On the other hand, without the addition of μισθόν it is difficult to take the genitives as expressing a reward. No theologian would deny that the social life of heaven is gentle, humane, and equitable, by contrast with life here below, but it is not now the fashion to call attention to this aspect of beatitude.

77 Plato says this often (in *Gorg.* 523e–524a, *Apol.* 41a, *Rep.* 615a, *Phaedr.* 249a). Justin has already used the point to the advantage of Christianity in 1 *Apol.* 8.4. Zeus was the father of Rhadamanthus in the legend. Athenagoras carries the contrast further by making Rhadamanthus and Minos liable to judgment themselves.

78 Found verbatim in 1 Cor. 15.32 and Isa. 22.13 (Sept.).

79 For Death and his brother Sleep, see *Iliad* 16.672. Plato, *Apol.* 40c, ridicules the idea that death can be a sleep. For the recurrence of the idea in Athenagoras, *De ress.* 16, see n. 62a to the same.

80 The sentence has become so complicated that πνεύματος which, I think, Athenagoras meant to go with the article τοῦ, has become widely separated from it and has picked up two other genitives, τοῦ παιδός and τοῦ πατρός, whether these are glosses or part of the original text. Bardy translates: 'Qui se laissent conduire par le désir de connaître le vrai Dieu,' but παραπεμπόμενοι ὑπὸ μόνου τοῦ εἰδέναι would be uncommon Greek and it seems impossible to get any idea

of desire out of the text. Richardson seems to suppose a gap in the text, for his version hardly makes sense.

81 Unity and sharing are concepts which Athenagoras has here for the first time applied to the theology of the Trinity. κοινωνία is not used by the Apostolic Fathers or Apologists in this connexion, though Plato's use of the term to apply to friendly numbers may have helped towards its Christian use. ἑνότης is a favourite word with Ignatius, but even in *Eph.* 14.1 and *Smyrn.* 12.2 the unity is rather of men with God than of the Persons of the Trinity among themselves. ἕνωσις and διαίρεσις are likewise proper to Athenagoras among Christians.

82 Matt. 5.46 and Luke 6.32, 34 are here conflated.

83 In Hippolytus, *Trad. apost.* 23.2, milk mixed with honey is given to the neophytes. There may have been some ceremonial tasting of these before the baptism ceremony began. Theophilus, *Ad Autol.* 2.12, has a similar comparison.

84 ἀθεώρητος is used of 'knowledge by acquaintance,' while ἀμαθής is rather for 'knowledge about' God. Athenagoras is unique among the Apologists in using ἀθεώρητος.

85 According to Diogenes Laertius (7.33.41) Cleanthes divided philosophy into six λόγοι or topics, of which the φυσικός and θεολογικός were fifth and sixth respectively. Thus the terms here used are standard.

86 Cicero, *De nat. deor.* 1.41.116, says: '*Est enim pietas iustitia adversum deos.*' The spirit of *do ut des* proper to Roman paganism could not be more clearly expressed.

87 The idea of God as the perfect fragrance is an idea found also in Irenaeus, *Adv. haer.* 4.25.3 H: '*Omnem odorem suavitatis et omnes suaveolentium vaporationes habens in se*'; but here it is used to show the superiority of Christian to Jewish sacraments.

88 The recently-found homily of Melito, 82 f. (Bonner), has a similar hymn of praise to the Demiurgos, the maker of the world. Jewish sources are there suggested for it and for the larger liturgical prayer on the same theme in *Const. apost.* 8.12.6–27 (Quasten). It is possible therefore that here also a liturgical preface is being drawn upon. The mention of 'pure hands uplifted by the Christians' (cf. 1 Tim. 2.8 and below) would then be most appropriate.

89 Geffcken and Schwartz suppose that an object has dropped out of the text after the participles συνέχοντα καὶ ἐποπτεύοντα, but τὰ πάντα can be put to double use, supplying an object here and to the verb ἄγει.

90 The Homeric passage, *Iliad* 9.499–501, is already used by Plato, *Rep.* 364d, as an example of the abuse of the truth about God.

⁹¹ Rom. 12.1 is alluded to here. Athenagoras cannot be said to deny that the Eucharist is a sacrifice. Indeed he has quite possibly (see n. 88) just been citing an eucharistic prayer, and without enlarging on the idea he could well include the Eucharist in the Pauline term λογικὴ λατρεία. The text is at this point almost certainly corrupt, as the editors all agree. I have translated it as it stands, but with some misgiving. Cicero, De nat. deor. 2.28.71, had already urged that pure praise of mind and voice was the best worship of God.

⁹² μάτην is rightly ejected from the text by Maran and by most subsequent editors.

⁹³ Celeus and Metaneira, king and queen of Eleusis, gave hospitality to Demeter when she was searching for Kore. The story was at the base of the Eleusinian mysteries: see Hom. hymn. ad Dem. 161 and 185–255; Pausanias 1.39.1; Nicander, Ther. 487. For some divine honours paid to the pair, see Pausanias 1.39.2.

⁹⁴ The temple of Menelaus at Sparta is mentioned by Pausanias 3.19.9 and Polybius 5.18.3. A. J. B. Wace and M. S. Thompson, Ann. Brit. School at Athens 15 (1908–9) 108, have excavated it fully. Isocrates, Enc. Hel. 63, shows that the Menelaus cult was really the worship of a deity and not merely of a hero.

⁹⁵ For the cult of Hector, see Dio Chrysostomus, Orat. Troi. 40.104, and Lucian, Deor. conc. 12; for the miracles, Philostratus, Her. 3.21.

⁹⁶ Aristaeus was in the legend (Apollonius of Rhodes 2.510–20) son of Apollo and Cyrene of Thessaly (see RE 2.853–59). In Boeotia he seems to have supplanted the cult of his father Apollo in certain shrines. Pindar in fr. 251 makes him to go from Ceos to Arcadia where he is worshipped as Zeus (cf. Aristotle, Κέων πολιτεία fr. 468). Apollonius Rhodius reverses this move. Cf. Roscher 1.547–51.

⁹⁷ Theagenes certainly had a statue at Thasos, for Pausanias saw it (6.6 and 11), and Athenaeus also vouches for it (32a). See also Athen. Mitt. 33 (1908) 234; Rev. étud. anc. 14 (1912) 377, 15 (1913) 31; IG 12.8.278 c31. Theagenes or Theogenes (cf. Roscher 5.538 f.), the son of a priest of Heracles, was a famous athlete. The fact of his having done murder at the Olympic games is not otherwise known, but if he killed his adversary in the pancratium, he might well have been described by a Christian as having done murder. The 'murder' done by his statue at Thasos, as told by Pausanias (6.11), is quite another story. It is just possible that Athenagoras has confused it with the athletic feats of the hero himself, but no one can say this with certainty.

⁹⁸ Lysander was the Spartan commander in the closing stages of the Peloponnesian war. Duris of Samos is the authority (cited in Plutarch, Lys. 18) for his cult in Samos, where he supplanted a festival of Hera.

⁹⁹ The honours paid to Niobe and Medea in Cilicia are unknown. The names of the poets Hesiod and Alcman are inscribed in the text here apparently as a gloss by some scribe who wanted to show where Niobe's story was told. Medea may well have been honoured in Colchis. Schwartz has added three more examples to the text of men who were honoured by local cults in antiquity, but there is no reason for thinking that Athenagoras would have approved of Schwartz's choice of examples.

¹⁰⁰ Butacides of Croton was the father of this Philip, who is known from Herodotus 5.47. He was an Olympic victor of renown and was honoured with a shrine and with sacrifices at his tomb in Segesta, a barbarian city.

¹⁰¹ Onesilaus: see Herodotus 5.104–114 for the story. In the early 5th century he besieged Amathus in Cyprus and was slain there. The Amathusians hung his head on their gates and a swarm of bees settled in it. An oracle then told them to honour him as a hero with an annual sacrifice.

¹⁰² Hamilcar, according to the story in Herodotus 7.167, threw himself into the fire as he learnt by divination that the Carthaginians had been defeated in Sicily in 480 B.C. He was honoured with sacrifices and monuments in Carthage and in all her colonies. In their *Commentary on Herodotus* How and Wells (*ad loc.*) suggest that he may have misunderstood the worship paid to Melcarth as being given to Hamilcar (Abd-Melqart). But Herodotus is usually accurate. It is probable that Athenagoras is using Herodotus direct.

¹⁰³ Egyptian worship was a stock joke in the early centuries A.D., (see even earlier, Cicero, *De deor. nat.* 1.36.101: 'qui inridentur Aegyptii . . .') though it was carried on and flourished in the centre of Rome (cf. Tacitus, *Hist.* 3.74; Juvenal, *Sat.* 6.526 ff. and *Sat.* 15).

¹⁰⁴ Xenophanes already (Plutarch, *De supers.* 171e, *De Is. et Osir.* 379b, *Amat.* 763d) had given the Egyptians this dilemma: If you weep for them, they are not gods: if you worship them as gods, you cannot weep for them.

¹⁰⁵ M. Aurelius (*Med.* 4.1) considered the divine power to pervade all material objects: 'It is like a fire, when it masters everything that falls into it, . . . leaping yet higher from the things that hinder it.'

¹⁰⁶ For pot and potter, see Rom. 9.21.

¹⁰⁷ Athenagoras is but elaborating here Paul's argument to the Areopagus (Acts 17.29). Paul said that the divinity could not be like things of gold and silver, fashioned by men's hands. Athenagoras extends the thought by stating that an analogy exists between man's creative activity and God's. The full theory of analogy of being, though foreshad-

10

owed in Plato, was to be perfected in the Cappadocians and Athanasius. Cf. P. Grenet, *Les origines de l'analogie philosophique dans les dialogues de Platon* (Paris 1948) passim.

[108] One may wonder whether paganism was ever so crude as to believe in the divine nature of statues; meteorites turned into statues are quite a different proposition. See also n. 136 below.

[109] Albinus, *Epit.* 15.1, states the contemporary Platonic case for worshipping the teeming divinities of the material universe: 'Now there are other spirits (δαίμονες) whom one might call created gods, shared out severally among the elements, some visible and others invisible, in sky and fire, in air and water. In fact no part of the material universe is without its share of a spiritual reality that is living with a life above that of mortal men.' This was the case that Athenagoras had here to answer.

[110] The beauty of the world is proclaimed by most philosophers, e.g. Ps.-Plutarch, *De plac. phil.* 1.6:879c ff.: Plato, *Tim.* 29a; Philo, *De praem. et poen.* 40–42, *De spec. leg.* 187–88, while to M. Aurelius beauty was an absolute (*Med.* 4.20). See L. Richter, *Philosophisches in der Gottes- und Logoslehre des Apologeten Athenagoras aus Athen* (Meissen, 1905).

[111] The phrase 'all in all' is found in 1 Cor. 15.28, 10.33, and Col. 3.11; also in Maximus of Tyre 32.4.

[112] The palace-simile is apt enough in such a discourse and is a philosophical commonplace: cf. Philo, *De decal.* 65 f.; Maximus of Tyre 17.12; etc.

[113] God's freedom in creating was a stumbling block to the Stoic, to whom the movement of creation was a biological urge as powerful as the sex instinct. 'The universe loves to create what is destined to be,' says Marcus Aurelius—*Med.* 10.21. Cf. also Euripides, *fr.* 898; Philo, *De cher.* 93–97, with the Christian reply in Minucius Felix 18.7 and Tertullian, *Adv. Prax.* 5.

[114] 1 Tim. 6.16 has the words φῶς ἀπρόσιτον of God's dwelling place. Athenagoras makes them a description of God's being. A whole metaphysic of light runs through Scholasticism, as distinct from a metaphysic of being. It is interesting to meet it so early in the story.

[115] For the comparison of the universe to a great lyre see the Neo-Pythagoreans Maximus of Tyre 19.3 and the author of the treatise *De mundo* 399 a14; Philo also, *De somn.* 1.35, has something of the same idea. Tertullian, *Ad nat.* 2.5.9, has drawn from it the same lesson as Athenagoras. Cicero in the *Somnium Scipionis*, using Greek sources, had plenty to say about the music of the spheres without being precise as to the instrument he favoured. According to Ps.-Plutarch, *De*

plac. phil. 1.6:880a, this harmony was used as an argument for the existence of God.

¹¹⁶ Plato, *Tim.* 33c, says that the world is the result of skilled craftsmanship—ἐκ τέχνης γέγονεν. This is enough to justify Athenagoras in saying that Plato had called it τέχνη θεοῦ. Bardy's doubts on the point are unjustified.

¹¹⁷ The Peripatetics are described (in Ps.-Plutarch, *De plac. phil.* 1.7:881 f, whom Athenagoras seems to be following here) as holding that each of the spheres is a composite formed out of body *and soul*. Substance, οὐσία, would hardly make sense here, on any estimate of the Aristotelian position, and I have therefore supposed the reading to be ψυχή rather than οὐσία of Geffcken's text. The change—for words written in uncials—is not so great as one might think.

¹¹⁸ The 'beggarly elements' are mentioned in Gal. 4.3, 4.9, and Col. 2.8, 2.20.

¹¹⁹ The Stoics (Ps.-Plutarch, *De plac. phil.* 1.7:881 f) proclaimed 'that God is intelligent, a creative fire, journeying forth to the creation of the world, embracing all those seminal principles according to which all things happen of necessity.' Thus the powers of God—δυνάμεις—are these λόγοι σπερματικοί of the Stoics. The treatise *De mundo* 398 a2 has very similar doctrine. M. Aurelius wrote of these powers (*Med.* 9.1.4) that they were fecund γόνιμοι.

¹²⁰ Plato is cited (*Pol.* 269d), obviously with approval. This fact, along with the sharp comments on the Peripatetics which precede, shows well enough Athenagoras's philosophical allegiance. The passage from Plato is used again by Eusebius, *Praep. evang.* 11.32.6.

¹²¹ The two authorities to consult on the history of classical art, into which Athenagoras plunges here, are H. S. Jones, *Select Passages from Ancient Writers, illustrative of the History of Greek Sculpture* (London 1895), and K. Jex-Blake–E. Sellers, *The Elder Pliny's Chapters on the History of Art* (London 1896). See also *Rhein. Mus.* NF 42 (1893) 522.

¹²² Herodotus 2.53. It is clear—as How and Wells point out—that Herodotus is giving his personal views on dating, not those commonly accepted in his time. His date for Hesiod may be accepted, but hardly that for Homer. Incidentally, Athenagoras's observation that the current information about the gods is of, 'as one might say, only the other day,' was then some six centuries old: he took it from Herodotus, *ibid.*

¹²³ Athenagoras has probably used some Alexandrine canon from a handbook on sculpture and painting. On the whole his information is better than that of Pliny.

124 Saurios certainly existed, but one may well doubt what exactly his σκιαγραφία was. Plato, *Rep.* 523b, 583b, etc., speaks of it as a form of painting in perspective, a painting with shadows such that the illusion of solidity was produced. This can hardly be what Athenagoras means.

125 Crato of Sicyon seems to have begun a technique of white-ground painting. Cleanthes of Corinth (Pliny, *Nat. hist.* 35.15) was his successor, being credited by Demetrius of Scepsis with the paintings of the Fall of Troy and of the Birth of Athena in the temple of Artemis at Olympia (cf. Strabo, 8.343 ; Athenaeus 346b). Pliny makes Cleanthes the discoverer of drawing in line (*linearis pictura*). Athenagoras must be quoting from a manual of Greek art composed before 146 B.C., and had probably never visited Corinth. If he was an Athenian, rather than an Alexandrian, this would be strange.

126 The story of the Corinthian maid is told by Pliny, *Nat. hist.* 35.151. She was the daughter of Boutades the potter of Sicyon, and traced out her lover's profile cast by lamplight upon a wall, just before he departed for a distant land. Her father filled in the outline with clay and then fired this model with his other pots. The finished work was kept at the Nymphaeum until the sack of Corinth in 146 B.C.

127 Daedalus's legend is in Pausanias (9.40.3), Pliny (*Nat. hist.* 7.198), and Diodorus Siculus (4.76). The story that he made statues which could move is in Suidas (s.v. Δαιδάλου ποιήματα). All that one need retain from all this is that he was an early and very skilful craftsman.

128 Smilis, son of Eucleides of Aegina, is known as the painter of the statue of Hera at Samos (Clement of Alexandria, *Protr.* 4.47.2, citing Olympichus). The statue was *in habitu nubentis* according to Lactantius, *Div. inst.* 1.17.8, and is figured on coins of Samos (*Brit. Mus. Cat. of Greek Coins: Ionia* [1892] pl. XXXVI.15 and XXXVII. 1, 2, 5, 6; also P. Gardner, *Samos and Samian Coins* [London 1882] pl. V.1–9). A date is assigned to him by Aethlius (Clement, *Protr.* 4.46.3), but all that seems safe is to place him in the early 6th century at the latest. Pliny (*Nat. hist.* 36.90) says that he was the architect along with Theodore of the labyrinth or Heraeum of Samos.

129 Athela: the word (ἀθήλη) might be regarded as an irregular form of ἄθηλος exempt from the ordinary rules for compounds of α-privative, and then it could mean 'not having been suckled at the breast,' which would provide an allusion to the legend of Athena's emergence full-grown from the head of Zeus. An alternative possibility (but see *Iliad* 2.547 f.) might be that the word meant 'not having given suck' and thus refer to the generally believed story of Athena's virginity. Pausanias tells (1.26.6) of an olivewood statue

of Athena, and in Herodotus 8.55 there is a story of an olivewood stump kept on the Acropolis as a sacred relic. It is not clear which is referred to here, but the text has probably suffered some dislocation. Geffcken suggests 'Αλέας and compares Pausanias 8.46.4 on Endoeus's statue of Athena Alea at Rome.

130 Pausanias credits Endoeus with the seated statue of Athena dedicated by Callias about 550 B.C. His name has been found (IG 1.2.978) on a statue base from the Acropolis. According to Pliny (Nat. hist. 16.213 f.) Endoeus chose vinewood as his material for a statue of Diana. The editors of Pliny use this passage of Athenagoras to correct the meaningless words eandem con of their MSS of Pliny into Endoeon.

131 The statue of the Pythian Apollo is listed in the inventory of Delos (Bull. de corr. hell. 6.128) and is copied on coins shown by J. N. Svoronos–B. Pick, Trésor des monnaies d'Athènes (Munich 1926) pl. LVI and LXXX.8.

132 Theodore was a Samian (cf. Herodotus 3.41; Diogenes Laertius 2.103), being an architect and sculptor in bronze. Pliny (Nat. hist. 7.198) makes him the inventor of rule and line, lathe and lever. He is said to have worked for Croesus and for Polycrates of Samos, thus belonging to the latter half of the 6th century B.C. Plato (Ion 533b) praised his bronze statuary. His Apollo Pythius in Samos (Diodorus Siculus 1.98.5) is said to have been made, one half by himself at Ephesus, and the other half by Telecles at Samos, both sections, right and left, being then put together as by a miracle.

133 Angelion and Tectaeus made the Delian Apollo (Pausanias 2.32.5). As this bronze statue was gilded (IG 9.2.287 B 66), it may be that one made the statue while the other did the gilding.

134 Praxiteles, a 4th-century Athenian, made the altar of Artemis at Ephesus after 356 B.C. His marble Aphrodite of Cnidos (Pliny, Nat. hist. 36.20) is represented on coins (see P. Gardner, Types of Greek Coins [Cambridge 1883] pl. XV. 21) and is described by Lucian (Imag. 6). He strove to render the emotions of his subjects, thus humanizing the gods.—It is puzzling to know what can be meant by 'another work of Praxiteles': if the text is changed from ἑτέρα to ἑταίρα as Maran proposed long ago, then we have a reference to the statue of Phryne the courtesan as Aphrodite which stood at Thespiae (Pausanias 9.27.5).

135 Phidias's most famous statue, the Athena Promachos, was made in 460–450 B.C., being followed (447–432) by the Parthenon sculptures, which he designed in clay and plaster for others to execute in the marble that remains to us. His experiments with statues of gold and ivory plates on a framework of wood (the Athena Parthenos and the Zeus

of Olympia) were world-famous in his lifetime but did not survive for long. Pausanias (2.27.2) says Thrasymedes made the Epidaurus statue.

136 The acceptance by some pagans at least of the idea that the statue was itself divine is vouched for by Plutarch (*De supers*. 167d), who speaks of the δεισιδαίμων or superstitious man worshipping statues of bronze or wood or wax. Doubtless this was not the case with pagans whose minds had been ennobled by the philosophy of Plato, but superstition, which led to magic, was more potent an influence in the 1st and 2nd centuries A.D. than the philosophy of Plato.

137 Celsus (Origen, *C. Cels*. 7.62) dismisses the idea of statues being gods as ridiculous, but, as remarked in the previous note, Plutarch shows that many pagans held it. The more intellectual attitude of men like Celsus has now to be met. The renewed appeal to the emperors, with its apology, serves to elevate the tone of the discourse after the forthright heckling of the last chapter.

138 *Iliad* 20.131.

139 The attitude of early Christians towards images of Christ and the saints is not often mentioned by the Fathers, yet they had such images, as the tombs under St. Peter's, Rome, with the 2nd-century picture of Christ as Helios, and the Christian paintings of Dura-Europos (early 3rd century) show. The *Clementine Recognitions* have a pagan who says: *Nos ad honorem invisibilis dei imagines visibiles adoramus*, but there is no sign that the Christians want to echo such sentiments. See further H. Leclercq, DACL 7.1 (1926) 15 and *ibid*. 182 and 194 s.vv. 'Iconographie,' 'Images.'

140 ἔχοιτε, a plain optative for a wish does not need the addition of ἄν, to make the sentence potential, as Bardy, after Geffcken, suggests. Nor is εἴθε required: Goodwin, *Greek Grammar* 1507.

141 *Thou shouldst not have any power against me unless it were given thee from above*, said Christ to Pilate (John 19.11); Athenagoras echoes the word ἄνωθεν, 'from above,' from John, admitting at the same time that the Christians recognize the imperial rule as legitimate, even though it persecutes them. Rom. 13.1 was not a dead letter.

142 Prov. 21.1. Athenagoras has changed the Jewish word 'heart' into the Greek ψυχή, soul.

143 νοουμένῳ is more naturally taken as a predicate of the Logos than as describing how men conceive the Logos as undivided from the Father, for in fact they do not do so; and, if that were the sense, it would be natural to expect ὡς in the text. Bardy's version, 'regardé comme inséparable de lui,' can hardly be correct. Richardson has followed Bardy.

[144] The reason why Athenagoras does not speak of the Holy Spirit here is perhaps a familiarity with what I have called two-member creeds: cf. *Early Christian Baptism and the Creed* (London 1950) 89–95.

[145] Plato, *Crat.* 402b, had said that the gods have a beginning. The account in Aristophanes, *Aves* 690–700, parodies the teaching of the sophists of the late 5th century on the subject. Night is there described as producing unaided the wind egg from which Eros comes forth.

[146] *Iliad* 14.201, also quoted by Plato in the passage referred to in n. 145.

[147] For the Orphic theogonies see now K. Ziegler, 'Orphische Dichtung,' RE 18.2 (1943) 1345–67; also M. P. Nilsson, *Geschichte der griechischen Religion* 1 (2 ed. Munich 1955) 678–99; the same in OCD s.v. 'Orphism.' The account Athenagoras gives is generally supposed to be nearer to that of Hellanicus and Hieronymus than to any other of the manifold Orphic genealogies. The name of Heracles added to that of Chronos for the original being is unusual. Night is absent from this account, though present as a primary factor in all other versions of Orphism, except in the syncretistic works of Hellanicus and Hieronymus: cf. Plato, *Crat.* 396 bc. For the cosmic egg, see M.-J. Lagrange, *Introduction à l'étude du Nouveau Testament IV: Critique historique* 1: *Les mystères: Orphisme* (Paris 1937) 122, 126.

[148] The text reads θεὸς γῆ διὰ σώματος. Conjecture seems fairly justified in the change to δισώματος, but the mention of Γῆ is more troublesome. Kern's choice of Μῆτις ἀσώματος carries weight as coming from the editor of the Orphic fragments, and in the Paris magical papyrus (*Die griechischen Zauberpapyri* 4.1777) Phanes is invoked as ἀσώματος, and in Damascius's account also, but as Athenagoras in 20 below speaks of the egg-produced Phanes as swallowed up by Zeus, he at least must have credited Phanes with a body. For emendations which remove the reference to Phanes in 20, see n. 166. There is on the other hand considerable evidence among Orphics for a double-sexed creature (similar to those of Plato, *Symp.* 190a) coming from the egg. See K. Preisendanz's article, 'Phanes,' RE 19.2 (1938) 1761–74. Lagrange, *op. cit.* 122, is perhaps inclined to take the cosmogony of Aristophanes too seriously and he struggles to explain how in the Orphic system Eros could be produced as the first-begotten of all beings and yet Phanes 'par une alternance de noms appliqués à la même personne' regarded by Orphics as first-begotten also. This is to take Greek comedy altogether too seriously. On the gold tablets from Sicily Γῆ is called πρωτόγονος.

[149] The Orphic theology, besides giving an account of the origin of the gods, which made them out to be the thinly disguised principles

of time, sky, earth, and light, included the story of man's origin. This was delivered through the myth of the Titans (cf. RE VI A2 [1937] 1491–1507).

150 *Orphica* fr. 19 (Abel). Cf. Hesiod, *Theog.* 207–210. The Orphic hymns do not date from much earlier than 200 B.C., though the *Marmor Parium* 264–63 B.C. gives Orpheus's date as being in the 14th century B.C. This means that the Greeks of the 3rd century regarded Orpheus as older than Homer. Plato, *Laws* 960c, ascribes the naming of the Three Fates, Clotho, Lachesis, and Atropos, to Hesiod.

151 The text is undoubtedly corrupt. Where the scribe of our single MS omits a whole line by haplography, we are helpless to reconstruct his omissions. The editors have rewritten the line each in his own way. In translating I have chosen to follow Gesner in reading ἐκεῖνο τοίνυν ⟨σκεπτέον⟩ and in making the words that follow into a question: ἕκαστον γὰρ τῶν τεθεολογημένων πῶς τὴν ἀρχὴν οὐκ ὂν εἶναι ⟨θεωρεῖται;⟩.

152 Cf. Plato, *Tim.* 27d. This text is twice used in Eusebius, *Praep. evang.* 11.2.4 and 11.10.10: once from Ps.-Justin, *Cohort.* 22, and once from Numenius. This speaks for its popularity in Christian writing.

153 Aristotle is not mentioned here, for he did not accept the immortality of the soul, and with his complicated system of prime movers for the spheres he would not have been of much help. Athenagoras passes on therefore directly to the Stoics.

154 2 Peter 3.10–13 was a description of the ἐκπύρωσις; Acts 3.21 mentions the ἀποκατάστασις πάντων, Matt. 19.28 has the παλιγγενεσία; but in all such places, as Justin, 1 *Apol.* 20.1–4, had already pointed out, there was no more than a similarity of Christian doctrine to the pagan. Technical terms can be interchanged between two systems without a full exchange of concepts; especially is this the case when the terms have lost their original sharpness of definition. For an account of Stoic physics, see A. H. Armstrong, *An Introduction to Ancient Philosophy* (London 1947) 122–25.

155 Philo reports (*De aetern. mun.* 83) that some Stoics were exercised about the position of God during the ἐκπύρωσις. See Armstrong, *op. cit.* 142 f., for the gradual dropping of this idea of the Conflagration by the Stoics.

156 I read ἀλλ' οὐδέ and τε with the MS and do not accept Schwartz's ἀλλ' οὔτε . . . γάρ . . . , as Geffcken does. In Plato, *Theaet.* 159e (see J. D. Denniston, *The Greek Particles* [Oxford 1934] 509), there is a parallel example of τε . . . οὔτε, and here the τε is planted in a virtually negative clause, as Greek usage requires. Athenagoras is therefore urging that the Stoics are inconsistent; they say that all comes from water, and on the other hand they argue that all things do not

come from water. Bardy has altered the sense, writing: 'Mais l'eau n'est pas, comme ils le disent, le principe de tout,' which is a misconstruction of κατ' αὐτούς on any reading of the text.

¹⁵⁷ ἐκτυπώματα. As Schwartz points out, the word is Platonic (*Tim.* 50d), being used to mean figures in relief.

¹⁵⁸ That matter should be older than God would seem absurd to any Stoic, for had not Chrysippus called Fate the προκαταρκτικὸς αἰτία (*Stoic. vet. frag.* 2.292)?

¹⁵⁹ Rhea or Demeter: see Hesiod, *Theog.* 912 f. who names Zeus and Demeter as parents of Persephone. From Euripides, *Hel.* 1301 ff., it is known that Rhea and Demeter were identified by some. Hence, though the text here is corrupt, it may be presumed that Athenagoras is alluding to this identification.

¹⁶⁰ The monstrous birth would be, Athenagoras implies, the just sequel of the unnatural act. Persephone is called horned in the Homeric hymn 19.11. Io was generally known to be afflicted from birth with abnormalities of this kind, but there is no other evidence than Athenagoras's for the plight of Persephone.

¹⁶¹ The title Athela (the unsuckled one) may have been used for Athena in 17 above. If so, it is natural for the author here to distinguish Persephone Athela from Athena.

¹⁶² The title Pallas Athena is generally derived from πάλλαξ = a maiden. A slight change (κόρρη for κόρη) would make Athenagoras derive the name Athena from her birth from the forehead (κόρρη) of Zeus.

¹⁶³ Ouranos was the father of Kronos, who must not be confused with the Chronos of 18 above.

¹⁶⁴ Seneca, *Ep.* 87.38, and Pliny, *Nat. hist.* 28.63 f., speak of the knot of Heracles. It is represented in the badge worn by doctors of the British Army Medical Service. It was commonly believed to have efficacy in certain maladies.

¹⁶⁵ κεκριμένος sometimes means what has been tried and found wanting and hence condemned, but it also means what has been tried and found worthy.

¹⁶⁶ The Orphic poem gives rise to great difficulties. Phanes is supposed by the Orphics to be the god who came from the egg. How then can he give birth (for τεκνοῦμαι is *regularly* used of the woman's part in procreation) from his sacred womb to this monster, even if he is two-bodied? Then too, the birth of Echidna is described in Hesiod, *Theog.* 295 ff., where the mother and father are Callirhoë and Chrysaor. In view of these difficulties, it has been proposed (cf. K. Preisendanz in RE 19.2. 1768) to read ἂν δὲ φανεῖσ' ἄλλην here, converting the

proper name Phanes into a participle. The error, if error it be, thus corrected must go back to a time before Athenagoras, for he certainly seems to have thought Phanes was mentioned in this fragment.

[167] The attack on the poets for their tales about the gods is as old as Plato, *Rep.* 377–91, and all subsequent Greek writers are more or less in his debt. He himself was not the first to criticize the official Pantheon. In his day there was the gentle criticism of Aeschylus that deepened the tales without removing their antinomies, and this Plato (*Rep.* 383 b) does not seem to have followed. Nor did the allegorizing of Anaxagoras appeal to him, as *Rep.* 378d shows. The anti-intellectual revival of devotion promoted by the Orphics, along with the cult of Minoan gods, cannot have claimed the whole of his heart, for Adeimantus is allowed to criticize them (363c), and Plato was too much of an intellectual to be finally happy in such company. There remains the downright iconoclasm of Xenophanes, and this seems to have been most after Plato's own heart; he was drifting loose from the ancient pagan pieties towards monotheism, the Orphic καθαρμός was sublimated, and only Apollo is treated with real respect (*Rep.* 427b, 461c, 540c).

Athenagoras has trodden the familiar way, but not without something of his own to contribute in matter and arrangement. When he breaks off his sentence with a rhetorical flourish, Geffcken and other editors have supposed that the sentence must have been finished, and have sometimes suggested how they would have completed it if they had been writing the *Embassy*. Such supplements are quite pointless. Plato had been inclined to treat Aeschylus with his own gentleness, not indeed approving but showing greater mildness to him than to some poets. Athenagoras has therefore to show that Aeschylus too is not a satisfactory theologian. As he follows Plato in a slight misquotation of Homer here, it is hard to deny, as Geffcken does, that he had been using Plato directly. If as is probable he had been a Platonic philosopher before becoming a Christian, there is no reason for arbitrarily denying that he could have read Plato and confining him to handbooks of extracts.

[168] The passages from the poets used by Athenagoras are given in the following list, based largely upon Geffcken, where parallels from other attackers of paganism are added in each case:

1. *Iliad* 4.23 f.—Athena and Hera: no parallels.
2. *Iliad* 22.168 f.—Pursuit of Hector: Josephus, *C. Ap.* 2.245; Heraclitus, *Alleg. Hom.* 42; Ps.-Justin, *Cohort.* 2.
3. *Iliad* 16.433 f., 16.522—Death of Sarpedon: Tertullian, *Apol.*

14. 3; *Ad nat.* 1.10.39; Clement, *Protr.* 4.55.3; Athanasius, *C. Gent.* 12; Firmicus Maternus 12.8.

4. *Iliad* 5.376, 858 ⎱ Aphrodite and Ares: Josephus, *C. Ap.* 2.245;
5. *Odyssey* 8.308 ff. ⎰ Tertullian, *Apol.* 14.3; Athanasius, *C. Gent.* 12; Clement, *Protr.* 2.36.1; Firmicus Maternus 12.8; Minucius Felix 24.7; Cyprian, *Quod idol.* 4.

6. *Iliad* 5.858—Wounding of Ares by Diomede: Clement, *Protr.* 2.36.1; Firmicus Maternus 12.8.

7. *Iliad* 15.605—Rage of Ares; no parallels.

8. *Iliad* 5.31—Ares, bane of men: Clement, *Protr.* 2.29.2.

9. *Iliad* 2.820 f.—Anchises and Aphrodite: Clement, *Protr.* 2.33.9; Firmicus Maternus 12.8.

10. *Iliad* 14.315–27—Zeus and Hera: Josephus, *C. Ap.* 2.246; Tertullian, *Apol.* 14.3; *Ad. nat.* 1.10.39; Ps.-Justin, *Cohort.* 2; Firmicus Maternus 12.4.

11. Euripides, *Alc.* 1 f., 8 f.—Apollo and Admetus: Josephus, *C. Ap.* 2.247; Philodemus p. 34.13; Lucian, *Iupp. conf.* 8; Clement, *Protr.* 2.35.1; Tertullian, *Apol.* 14.4; Minucius Felix 24.5.

12. Aeschylus, Fr. 350—Apollo and Hyacinth: Lucian, *Deor. dial.* 14; Tatian, *Orat.* 8; Theophilus 1.9; Clement, *Protr.* 2.33.5.

13. Aeschylus, *ibid.*—Apollo and Achilles: Plato, *Rep.* 383b.

---

[169] The speaker of these lines (*Odyssey* 8:308 f.) is Hephaestus. There is no reason for supposing with Richardson that Athenagoras means to say that it is Hephaestus who is wounded. Ares is smitten by love for Aphrodite and Hephaestus reports the fact.

[170] The death of Styx in battle is not recorded in extant classical literature—a warning that Athenagoras may have had better sources than those at our command.

[171] Aeneas, born of a human father and a goddess mother, excited little attention in Greek mythology, but was sufficiently well-established to warrant his choice as hero by Vergil. Perhaps it is a passing thought of Vergil here that prompts Athenagoras to turn aside from his theme to Christ, God and man, who was like unto us in all things, sin alone excepted.

[172] The word οἰκονομία began to be used in Ignatius, *Eph.* 18.2 and 20.1, and was by now an established term for the Incarnation.

[173] The myth of the death of Hyacinth at the hands of his lover Apollo is used against the pagans by Theophilus 1.9 and in the Acts of Achatius 2.4 (Krüger).

[174] Empedocles of Acragas began this identification of personal gods with the principles of the physical universe, perhaps under Orphic

influence (cf. Armstrong, *op. cit.*, 15). His four 'roots' or passive elements were combined by Love (Philia) or Aphrodite, and driven asunder by Strife (Neikos) or Ares.

175 Theophrastus maintained that Hera should be identified with the air on Empedocles's system, as against Crates of Mallos who made her the earth: cf. E. Wellmann in RE 5.2 (1905) 2509. There was as much confusion among ancient philosophers about these identifications as there was among the Fathers about the symbols of the four Evangelists (cf. H. Leclercq, DACL 5.1 [1922] 845 ff.).

176 Derivations of the names of the gods from common nouns or adjectives is practised by Plato in the *Cratylus*. He has this derivation of Hera from the noun meaning air (ἀήρ) by a process of rapid repetitions (αηραηραηρα), though he gives an alternative derivation from ἐρατή = 'the loved one' (*Crat.* 404c).

177 The derivations of Zeus and Poseidon are not recorded elsewhere —cf. n. 43 above. Poseidon may have been formed out of πόσις, meaning 'lord and master,' which is perhaps what Athenagoras meant.

178 For Zeus as a sky god, see M. P. Nilsson in OCD s.v.

179 ἡ τῆς ὕλης ἀλλαγή. The phrase means almost exactly what Whitehead called the 'passage of nature,' but as it stands in the text it cannot be construed, for there is no room for it as a nominative. I have followed Gesner's change of ἴσα to ὅσα, which puts the phrase inside a relative clause and is the simplest of many corrections.

180 The argument is directed against the theory that all pagan divinities are one god in many shapes. The πνεῦμα τοῦ θεοῦ would be more accurately called ψυχή. Marcus Aurelius (*Med.* 6.43) expressed something of this Stoic idea by saying that though the providence of each of the gods is different, they are all working to the same end. Far from being muddled, as Geffcken thinks, Athenagoras seems to be addressing his arguments to the correct destination.

181 The argument resembles that of Boethus of Sidon and other Stoics who denied the ἐκπύρωσις for the pertinent reason (cf. Philo, *De aeter. mund.* 83) that they could not see what happened to Zeus or to the world soul during the conflagration.

182 This rationalization of the myth of Kronos's castration was apparently known to the Orphics. Something very like the equation of the madness of a god to the change of the seasons is found as early as the Ugaritic poems, where Baal, rider of the clouds, smites down Yamm in berserk rage.

183 In listing these further alternatives, darkness, ice, and moisture, Athenagoras shows that he is aware that there are other forms of cos-

mological belief in which Night is a principal goddess (as in Aristophanes's *Aves*) or in which water rather than fire is the first principle of nature.

184 The derivation of Athena from Ἠθονόη or the right understanding of virtue (ἦθος, νόησις) is suggested by Plato, *Crat.* 407b. This would justify φρόνησις here.

185 The death of Osiris, who was cut in pieces by his brother Typhon (Set) and gathered together again by Isis, his sister-bride, was one of the chief articles of Egyptian faith. See Plutarch, *De Is. et Osir.* 13–19; Herodotus 2.41 f. and 62; Firmicus Maternus 2.6. Cf. Juvenal, *Sat.* 8.29 f: *Exclamare libet populus quod clamat Osiri invento.*

186 The MS has περὶ πελώρου as two words; I have taken these as one, for though a compound adjective περιπέλωρος is not found elsewhere, such compounds of emphasis are common in Greek, especially in the colloquial language (e.g. περιπληθής, περίμετρος).

187 Plato, *Crat.* 406c, derives the name of Dionysus from διδούς + οἶνος, the giver of wine. Athenagoras has apparently added on his own the parallel between the flaming heat of the sun that matures the grape and the thunderbolt wherewith Zeus smote Semele.

188 Europa's children Sarpedon and Minos were Cretans (Herodotus 1.173). The bull figures largely in Cretan mythology, but even Herodotus (4.45) did not know how this obscure goddess came to give her name to the continent.

189 Leda was mother of Apollo and Artemis by Zeus.

190 I accept the MS text. Myths are divinized when their content is transposed in terms of earth and air.

191 The doctrine of sympathy and of insight by sympathy was at the root of much ancient magic. Hence Athenagoras is using the idea (οὐ γὰρ ἔχουσιν συμπάθειαν) metaphorically.

192 The helmsman analogy is certainly Stoic (cf. Boethus of Sidon quoted by Philo, *De aetern. mund.* 83: πηδαλιουχεῖ τὰ σύμπαντα). In the absence of a rudder (not invented until the 11th century) ancient ships were guided by one or two paddles attached to the stern. Athenagoras clearly wants to regard the ship as pilotless, hence ἄγοι must mean 'consider' and not 'steer' and εἶναι must be supplied. Bardy, with 'le passage qui conduirait . . .' seems to be wrong. The comparison is not meant to suggest that without God the world would 'get along' in a poor sort of way, but that it would not get along at all. Ancient pilots cannot have been so very expert that a private person would necessarily have been considered worse than no pilot at all. The analogy reappears in Theophilus 1.8 and Athanasius, *C. Gent.* 39, but in neither place is it more than hinted at.

193 Athenagoras takes the line that diabolical miracles are not impossible, but that they can be shown not to be divine (otherwise, of course, God would be allowing us to be led into inevitable error). This is now the traditional line of Catholic apologetics (cf. St. Thomas, *Quaest. de malo* 16.9 f.), but it is hard to find it clearly expressed by any writer prior to Athenagoras. Tatian (18.2 f.) is perhaps independent of Athenagoras. He refers to Justin for the idea that diabolical possession was a cause of disease by a kind of holding-to-ransom; when the ransom was paid in the form of worship of the devil, then he let the victim go. Minucius Felix 27, Tertullian, *Apol.* 22, and Cyprian, *Quod idol.* 7, follow suit, but Irenaeus, *Adv. haer.* 2.48.2 H, was not so sure about this argument.

194 Thales was obviously not directly accessible to Athenagoras. Greek tradition is clear that he left no written works. That Athenagoras should himself mention the fact entitles us to suppose—till the contrary be proved—that when he quotes Plato and others, he had direct access to their works. Geffcken thinks he has proved that Athenagoras used not Plato himself, but a book of extracts from Plato, when he has shown that the text of Athenagoras's quotations agrees with that of Clement and Eusebius in their quotations rather than with our MSS of Plato. The balance of the evidence is however not decisive in favour of Geffcken's view. The first three words that show any textual variant in the present passage (*Tim.* 40de) are thus attested:

ἑαυτῶν Athenagoras, Clement, Eusebius	γε αὐτῶν Plato
εἰδότων Athenagoras, Clement	εἰδόσιν Plato, Eusebius
λέγωσιν Athenagoras	λέγουσιν Plato, Clement, Eusebius

Phenomena such as these do not point to Geffcken's conclusion at all. Further, the sentence of *Tim.* 41a which follows immediately upon the present extract, has been quoted by Athenagoras in 5 above, where he produced a reading (ἐμοῦ μὴ θέλοντος) which is supported by Athenaeus and the Latin version by Cicero against all our present MSS of Plato. All that one could safely conclude would be that in the 2nd century, as the papyri are beginning to make clear to us, there was far less fixity of text even in such important writers as Plato than used to be supposed in the days when Geffcken was writing and when the flood of papyri had only just begun.

195 This Milesian division into gods, spirits, and heroes is in keeping with the desire to have intermediaries between the gods and men which was still manifest in Asia Minor in the days of St. Paul: Col. 1.16 and 2.18.

¹⁹⁶ Phorcys was son of Nereus and Earth in Hesiod, *Theog.* 237. He was fabled to be father of the Gorgons and Sirens.

¹⁹⁷ I have read with the MS νοῦν rather than Schwartz's correction νῷ, which seems to have nothing in its favour.

¹⁹⁸ The extract is from Plato *Epist.* 2.312e. The words τῶν καλῶν, which in Plato's text limit the creative activity to what is beautiful, have here been omitted.

¹⁹⁹ Plato, continuing *ibid.*, is quite clearly speaking in riddles to Dionysius and there seems little point in trying to resolve them now. Justin, 1 *Apol.* 60.5, took him to mean that he had read the Pentateuch and had there found some vague knowledge of the Trinity. Clement of Alexandria, *Strom.* 5.14.103, follows Justin on the point. That Athenagoras does not, is a sign of his superior critical judgment.

²⁰⁰ Where exactly Plato says that it is impossible, is not mentioned by Athenagoras, but he may be thinking of *Rep.* 390c on the incontinence of the gods, or *Laws* (bk. 10), or perhaps *Phaedr.* 245. The following extract is from *Phaedrus* 246e.

²⁰¹ Seneca, *Nat. quaest.* 2.45, has this same distinction between Jove-in-the-Capitol and Jove ruler of-the-universe.

²⁰² In 21 the case for the gods being human was considered, in 22 that they were material, and in 23 that they were spirits. Now comes the summing-up.

²⁰³ The Platonic philosophy left its disciple in some uncertainty whether the Form of the Good (the highest of the Forms) was also a soul. Hence Athenagoras has settled for the idea that God, the highest soul, *has* goodness as an inseparable asset, rather than that God *is* goodness. The view of Aquinas (*Summa* 1a.6.3) that God is good by His very essence is not quite the same.

²⁰⁴ The devil is not described as the adversary of God by any Christian writer prior to Athenagoras, though in 2 Cor. 4.4 St. Paul calls Satan god of this world, and the name Slanderer which is commonly his in the Greek scriptures, implies the fuller title.

²⁰⁵ The spirit that busies itself with matter is thought of in the same way as in Philo, *De gig.* 6, where there are said to be some spirits for the earth, others for the water, etc. Philo, *De conf. ling.* 176 f. had written vaguely that all spiritual creatures are free from evil, ἀμέτοχοι κακίας; but in the passage first cited he has the whole story of the fornicating angels, declaring it to be no myth but a physical fact, seeing that the earth has its demons, fire its own, and so on. In the *Apocalypsis Petri* (p. 12 Klostermann) and in magical writers one meets with a spirit-guard described as τημελοῦχος ἄγγελος, and hell-guarding or ταρταροῦχος (cf. M. R. James in JTS 12 [1911] 573–83). That

Athenagoras, unlike Clement, should have kept away from these aberrations is all to his credit.

206 Geffcken here inserts in the text a passage which Epiphanius (*Haer.* 64.20) quotes as coming from Athenagoras, but as it contains at least three hapax legomena for the Apologists and Apostolic Fathers (κῦρος, ἀνηρτημένος, διευθύνων), it is probably due to some later writer, and I have omitted it.

207 The freedom of the angels is traditional Catholic doctrine, from Jude 6 onwards. See Justin, 2 *Apol.* 7.5.

208 The watchers who have sinned with the daughters of men and their giant offspring are mentioned in *Jubilees* 4.22 and 5.1–9 (Charles). Enoch is said to have testified against them. That they were the guardians of the first firmament is apparently not said elsewhere. That the guardians of the lowest sphere sinned while those of the higher spheres remained faithful would be a natural inference and would tend to restrict the effects of their sin to the lower orders of nature. In Plato, *Tim.* 34c and 46e, there is the idea that a surd element must exist in nature which could easily be interpreted by a Christian Platonist as being due to the vagaries of the fallen angels. The account of the sin of the angels here given is more complicated than J. Daniélou supposes it to be in *Les anges et leur mission* (Chevetogne 1953) 63.

209 The prophets were held to include Moses as their chief (Deut. 18.15) and hence Gen. 6.1–4, which is the source of the myth about the fornicating angels, might be said to come from the prophets.

210 The spirit in charge of matter is here clearly set apart from the fornicators. One can see that Athenagoras, by using John 12.31 and 14.30, has been able in part to shake himself free from Jewish mythology.

211 Hesiod, *Theog.* 27. Bardy takes it that Satan inspired Hesiod to write his poems: 'L'apologiste cite Hésiode sous le nom de prince de la matière, comme si le poète avait été inspiré par le diable.' This is rather hard on Hesiod and not at all necessary. The one wisdom is said to be heavenly, the other earthbound and under the rule of matter. The quotation is then added as an independent sentence. κατά with the accusative can certainly mean *according to X* (in his works), but the way the phrase ought to be taken here is roughly this: it replaces an adjective which would be parallel to τῆς ἐπιγείου. Bardy, whom Richardson follows, would have some difficulty in proving that Hesiod was in league with the prince of darkness.

212 Geffcken sees in ὑπερουράνια a reminiscence of Plato, *Phaedr.* 247c.

213 The principle underlying the discussion here is that action is in

keeping with the nature of one's being. Demons (i.e. disembodied giants, cf. *Enoch* 15.11) produce (perhaps in themselves and certainly in others) motions similar to their nature as giants, violent and unruly. Fallen angels however do not revert to their angelic nature nor act according to it after their sin, but remain fixed in evil (as a Scholastic theologian might say), and in them nature does not assert itself again. Stoicism had a rich demonology and this naturally excited similar speculations among Christians.

²¹⁴ Such good or ill success may have silenced some poets, but it has moved others to utterance; cf. G. M. Hopkins: 'Why do the wicked prosper?' The verse quoted is not found in any surviving play of Euripides (=fr. 901 Nauck); the verse following is from an unknown poet (=fr. 99 Nauck).

²¹⁵ Aristotle is here accused of what Geffcken claims the author of the *De mundo* to be guilty, but in his *De part. anim.* 641 b 19 he does say something nearly akin to what is condemned here: 'Order and definition is found rather in the heavens than in our sublunary world.'

²¹⁶ Euripides, *Cycl.* 332 f. Geffcken thought that Athenagoras could not have read the *Cyclops* of Euripides because the context of his quotation is inept to his purpose. But quotations that despoil the Egyptians and turn their own maxims against them are not unknown in patristic writing.

²¹⁷ 'Law of reason' (νόμῳ λόγου) is probably the correct reading. The essential rationality of nature was the later Stoic view, for to them reason pervaded the whole of the universe. Once the idea of the universal conflagration had been dropped, the idea of an all-controlling Providence emerged the more strongly.

²¹⁸ The phrase 'from within'=by possession, which antiquity recognized for a fact; 'from without,' that is, by enticements and spells. If men are more earth-bound, they respond to such controls more easily; if their souls are open to the divine influence, they answer less readily to these promptings.

²¹⁹ These were the Epicureans, who held that the *clinamen* (Lucretius 2.292) which guided the random atoms of the void into groups and clusters was something quite irrational, an irruption of an indeterminacy principle into their ordered science.

²²⁰ Disposition (διάθεσις) in Plato (*Phil.* 11d; *Rep.* 489b) is a mental rather than a physical quality. Accordingly I have given it that sense here, for Athenagoras is much addicted to Platonic terms. Bardy, with 'sa constitution physique qui ne transgresse pas la loi à laquelle elle est soumise,' makes one wonder if Athenagoras thought all men equally healthy. On the other hand, a spiritual disposition which

according to the nature of man (κατὰ τὴν πλάσιν) did not transgress its law, would be no more than conscience.

221 In the philosophic dispute between the Stoic Timocles and the Epicurean Damis in Lucian's *Zeus tragoedus* (51), Timocles is made to argue thus: If there are altars, there are gods also. But there are altars, ergo. It is this topic that Athenagoras now considers.

222 Tertullian, *Apol.* 23.14, repeats this argument from the sacrifices to the nature of the gods: *Renuntiant se immundos spiritus esse quod vel ex pabulis eorum, sanguine et fumo et putridis rogis pecorum, . . . intellegi debuit.*

223 The part demons play in oracles and divination generally is emphasized by the contemporary Platonist Albinus, *Epit.* 15.2.

224 The mutilation carried out in the worship of Cybele (who was identified with Rhea) is the theme of Catullus, *Carmen* 63. Cf. F. Cumont, *Les religions orientales dans le paganisme romain* (4. ed. Paris 1929) 47 f., 54 f. and nn. Seneca, *Fr.* 34, complains of such practices: *Ubi iratos deos timent, qui sic propitios merentur*: 'What are they going to do when the gods are angry, if they perform acts like this to win their favour?'

225 The Ephesian Artemis is probably referred to—cf. Roscher 1.591.

226 The insertion here of a mention of the Artemis of the Tauric Chersonese, who demanded human sacrifice, as in Euripides, *Iphigenia in Tauris*, is probably a gloss. I have followed Schwartz in bracketing it.

227 Flagellation and self-laceration in the manner of oriental fakirs was also practised in worships now domiciled in the West: see H. Graillot, *Le culte de Cybèle, Mère des Dieux, à Rome et dans L'Empire* (Paris 1912) 296; F. J. Dölger, *Ant. u. Christ.* 1 (1929) 176 f., 6 (1950) 311 f.

228 That Athenagoras should break off in disgust before finishing his sentence is quite natural. That critics should try to finish it for him, is not.

229 The saying (which resembles the Latin tag, *Quem Deus vult perdere, prius dementat*) is quoted by the scholiast to Sophocles's *Antigone* 620, and is from some unknown Greek tragedy (=*Fr. adesp.* 455 Nauck).

230 That demons really indwelt statues of the gods was professed by such passages as Ps.-Apuleius, *Asclep.* 37.

231 The statue of Nerullinus at Troas is quite unknown. Tacitus, *Ann.* 12. 25 and 13.43, speaks of one M. Suillius who took the cognomen Nerullinus in honour of Nero and who was consul in 50 A.D. and proconsul in Asia about 69–70 (cf. RE IV A 1 [1931] 719). It may be that his son or grandson (who seems to be mentioned on a coin

of Hierapolis) was honoured by a statue in a town which came under his rule as proconsul, but nothing is known of the doings of the descendents of M. Suillius. Maran's correction of the present ἐνεργεῖ into an imperfect seems right, and implies that the Nerullinus in question was dead at the time of writing.

232 For Alexander, see OCD s.v. 'Alexander of Abonuteichos'; also A. D. Nock, 'Alexander of Abonuteichos,' *Class. Qu.* 22 (1928) 160–63. This Alexander was a charlatan who set up in business as a prophet at Abonuteichos in Paphlagonia and founded a flourishing trade in oracles. The account of him by Lucian, *Alexander the Oracle-Monger*, making him the counterpart of a newspaper magnate, is almost our only evidence for his life. Though Athenagoras does not say that it is this Alexander he is talking about, it is usual to accept the identification. The only other candidate is Homer's Paris (also called Alexander), but as Nerullinus is a modern man for Athenagoras, it is hardly likely that he would be linked with an ancient figure. On the other hand, the word ἔτι used of Alexander's tomb at Parium is unusual if applied to a man who was still alive in the reign of M. Aurelius and who (Lucian *Alex.* 48) gave an oracle advising Marcus how he might win success in his war with the Marcomanni (173–4). Even if he died soon after, he would have been dead for no more than three years at the time of writing. Evidence for Paris having been educated at Parium has been found in Suidas (s.v.) and in John of Antioch (FHG 4.550). With the Homeric citation also in his favour, one must admit that Paris is the more suitable candidate and that Athenagoras is using a geographical rather than an historical principle of selection. It might be, as Eberhardt, p. 54 n. 1, suggests, that he is thinking primarily of Paris but sees the other Alexander as a pale parody of the Trojan.

233 Proteus is the famous Peregrinus (Lucian, *De morte Peregrini*) who threw himself into the fire at the Olympic games of 165 A.D. after a life of about sixty-five years, during part of which he had been a Christian in Palestine. Parium figured in his story as his birthplace, to which he withdrew temporarily when he had abandoned Christianity. See L. Baur, 'Peregrinus (genannt Proteus)' in LTK 8 (1936) 82.

234 The adjective ἐπήκοος is applied to Asclepius in an inscription of Thasos (cf. IG XII [8] 366).

235 Amasis (Herodotus 2.172) made a golden footpan into a statue which the Egyptians reverenced greatly. They were shocked to learn what it had previously been; whereupon Amasis pointed out that he himself had been of lowly origin but was now their king and they must

obey him. The story was welcomed by Christians as bringing pagan gods into contempt—cf. Justin, 1 *Apol.* 9.2; Minucius Felix 22.4.

236 The philosophy of idol-mongering is now discussed. The Egyptian statues of Memnon sometimes gave forth sounds at dawn (now thought to have been produced by the sudden access of the heat of the rising sun, which caused expansion of some of the parts, accompanied by friction and sounds like groans or threats) and the names of some of those who came and heard Memnon are still inscribed on these statues: cf. CIL 3.1.30–66. See also Strabo 17.1.46; Pliny, *Nat. hist.* 36.58; Tacitus, *Ann.* 2.61 (with Nipperdey's note); also RE 15.1 (1931) 648 f. Phenomena of this kind require a philosophical explanation, which Athenagoras now proceeds to give.

237 The psychology is mainly that of the Stoics: cf. Diogenes Laertius 7.45 f.; Philo, *De praem. et poen.* 17–19; also Armstrong 143 f.

238 The 'spirit of the material world is the intermediary between mind and matter.' Man was, according to Marcus Aurelius, *Med.* 12.3, made up of body, spirit, and mind, and only man's mind was really himself. Chrysippus said that seed, including human semen, was πνεῦμα (Diogenes Laertius 7.159), or spiritual, offering as proof the fact that seeds which are dried up are useless because their 'spirit' has evaporated.

239 There is an attempt here by Athenagoras to introduce some Christian elements into this psychology, and thus one meets with one of the first attempts at Christian philosophy. The term 'flesh and blood' is distinctly reminiscent of Matt. 16.17 and John 1.13 and is not Stoic at all.

240 ἐναποσφραγίσηται: the word is marked by Schwartz as Stoic, and from the example he gives (Sextus Empiricus, *Hyp.* 2.4) it supposes the *tabula rasa* view of the mind.

241 The word 'manipulating' (ἐπιβατεύειν) is properly applied to mariners handling a ship. Such trickery as was practised by Alexander of Abonuteichos (who masqueraded as the god Asclepius, with a tame serpent to perform his tricks) and such natural phenomena as those of the Memnon statues, would be instances of this manipulation.

242 That some prophecy is natural is admitted by Aquinas (2a–2ae. 172.1), who follows Plato here, as Athenagoras has obviously done.

243 Whether the phrase about 'healing present ills' covers miracles in the strict sense may be doubted. The Greek words are very noncommittal, and Athenagoras seems rather to mean that the devils take the credit for the work of doctors who cure by natural remedies.

244 This was Alexander the Great, but his letter was a forgery pro-

duced by Leon of Pella (cf. FHG 2.331 f. and RE 12.2 [1925] 2012 ff.).
Leon is cited under his own name by Clement of Alexandria, *Strom.*
1.21.106.3, and Tertullian, *De cor.* 7. Tatian, *Orat.* 27, says that if
the Greeks accepted the 'debunking' of their gods which Leon practised, they could not complain if Christians did the same.

²⁴⁵ Herodotus 2.144. Athenagoras's frequent use in this section of
Herodotus 2 is a sign of his good judgment and can hardly be explained
by supposing that he had before him a popular manual of atheism
with extracts from that source.

²⁴⁶ Herodotus is the authority (2.50) for saying that the Greeks
derived the names of most of their gods from Egypt. Modern research
is inclined to accept this, at least in the sense that Egypt influenced
Crete and that Minoan Crete influenced the Greeks. The story of
Aeschylus's *Supplices* and its chorus of Egyptian maidens is a clear
representation of this Egyptian influence on Greece.

²⁴⁷ Herodotus 2.156. The desire to find equivalents in one national
mythology for the gods of another was widespread in later antiquity.
Plutarch, writing of *Isis and Osiris* (351 f.), claims Isis as Greek. In
363e he goes further and bases both beliefs on cosmology, making
Osiris the Nile and Isis the land of Egypt.

²⁴⁸ Herodotus 2.41. Some Greeks said that Isis was daughter of
Prometheus, confusing her with Io, but Athenagoras does not fall into
this trap.

²⁴⁸ᵃ Herodotus 2.3.

²⁴⁹ Hermes Trismegistus is the Greek version of the Egyptian god
of letters, 'Thoth the Very Great,' and supposed author of the *Corpus
Hermeticum*; on which see the edition by W. Scott (Oxford 1924–36)
and that by A. D. Nock and A. J. Festugière (Paris 1945). This is probably the earliest reference to the *Corpus Hermeticum*, though Philo of
Byblos, writing in the time of Hadrian, has some knowledge of a
cosmogony of Thoth.

²⁵⁰ The MS reads ἀΐδιον. Schwartz corrected it to ἴδιον. There
is no verb in the subordinate clause, as the text stands, but only a
participle. It is therefore possible that a wider corruption of text has
taken place. In the meantime the translation I have given supposes
that the participle συνάπτων masks some form of indicative verb.
This yields a satisfactory sense. The argument then becomes: Alexander (cited above) and the Hermetic writings accept the immortality
of those gods which none the less they know to be men. If they accept
it, then everyone else will, (as these two have great wisdom, and) as
the god-men are kings anyhow and thus set apart from men.

²⁵¹ Apollodorus's περὶ θεῶν was a well-known philosophical

handbook of agnostic tendency produced about 150–120 B.C. It is lost, but was much used by the Apologists.

252 Herodotus 2.61. Athenagoras has used an emended text of Herodotus here. The best MSS of Herodotus now available have τὸν δὲ τύπτονται: 'whom they do mourning for' (the accusative *ad sensum* being retained with the passive), whereas Athenagoras has supplied τρόπον to make the accusative adverbial. Bardy and others translate the modern text of Herodotus, without regard to what Athenagoras had before him.

253 Commenting on the present text from Herodotus (2.170 f.), How and Wells say that the frequency of graves of Osiris in Egypt is due to the fact that his cult had swallowed up local cults by a process of syncretism, but the opposite explanation (that the villagers wanted their own Osiris shrine like the big one at Sais) would be more true to human nature.

254 The lake at Delos, still to be seen in its ancient 'hoop-like' wall, is described in RE 4.2 (1901) 2471.

255 Herodotus 2.86. Egyptians believed that the Ka or soul lived on only if the body was preserved naturally or by embalming. To be embalmed after the manner of Osiris was to ensure that your soul went to the kingdom of Osiris after death.

256 *Odyssey* 21.28. Heracles was the god most cherished by the Stoics (cf. Seneca, *Dial.* 2.2.1).

257 Hesiod, Fr. 125 (Rzach). Asclepius was slain for raising a dead man to life (cf. Roscher 1.619). Justin, 1 *Apol.* 21.1 f., makes his death a proof that paganism was familiar with the idea of a god who died and went to heaven. Aristides (10.5) comments that if Asclepius could not help himself, it is not likely that he will be able to help others. Athenagoras shows more discrimination than either by going to the cause of Zeus's anger with him, his greed of gold, which is a most ungodlike quality. I have accepted the correction (of Φοίβῳ for φίλον) made by Wilamowitz in the passage from Hesiod.

257a Pindar, *Pyth.* 3.54 f., 57 f.

258 The fragment of Euripides is said to come from his *Danaides* (fr. 324 Nauck).

259 The legend of Castor and Pollux (Polydeuces) as witnessed to by Homer certainly makes them mortals (*Il.* 3.243; *Od.* 11.301). The first evidence of their cult, under the title of Διόσκουροι, is an inscription from Thera (IG Ins. 3.359) of the 8th or 7th century B.C. Castor was said (Plutarch, *Quaest. graec.* 23) to be buried at Argos, while Polydeuces was honoured with a temple near Therapne (Pausanias 3.20.1).—For the man-god Amphiaraus, cf. OCD s.v.

²⁶⁰ Ino, wife of Athamas, and her son Melicertes (= Palaemon), died by a fatal leap into the sea while she was trying to save her son from her husband's murdering hands. For these as well as the case of Castor and Pollux, see Augustine, *De Civ. Dei* 18.14. The anonymous bits of verses following are known only from Athenagoras.

²⁶¹ Semiramis, daughter of Derceto, was exposed at birth. She was cared for by doves, and hence the dove was sacred to her. Sammuramat, regent of Assyria (810–805), may be the human figure behind this mythology.

²⁶² Derceto or Atargatis (the divine Ata) was the goddess of Hieropolis in Syria. Fish were sacred to her because she was believed to have fallen into a lake and to have been saved by the fish (or alternatively to have been changed into a fish; for the Syrians and the sacred fish, see Xenophon, *Anab.* 1.4.9, Cicero *De nat. deor.* 3.15.39, etc.; especially too the study by F. J. Dölger, ΙΧΘΥΣ: *Der heilige Fisch in den antiken Religionen und im Christentum* 2 [2 ed. Münster I. W. 1928] 161–75). She was sometimes portrayed as half-maiden, half-fish. Nero adopted her cult and its traces have been found even in Roman England. Ctesias was probably not used directly by Athenagoras as almost all his works perished at an early date.

²⁶³ At *Phaedr.* 244b.

²⁶⁴ *Orac. Sibyll.* 3.108–113. The Sibyl was popular with the Apologists and the corpus of Sibylline oracles suffered many a Christian interpolation (see OCD s.v. *Sibylla*), until eventually Raphael painted his famous character-studies of the four Sibyls. For the very extensive literature on the Sibyllines, cf. J. Quasten, *Patrology* 1 (1950) 169 f.

²⁶⁵ Antinous, Hadrian's boy favourite, after his death by drowning in the Nile (ca. A.D. 130) was deified by the lonely emperor. Marcus Aurelius himself, when he was six years old, had been noticed by Hadrian, who nicknamed him Verissimus (A.D. 127) and who arranged later to have him betrothed to the daughter of L. Ceionius Commodus, whom Hadrian desired to have as his successor. From the way in which Marcus praises Antoninus Pius by contrast with Hadrian (*Med.* 1.16.2) one gathers that he would not have approved of Antinous.

²⁶⁶ Callimachus, *Hymn. in Iov.* 8 f. In the same poem Callimachus spoke of Zeus's birth on Mt. Ida, and Athenagoras clearly knows this, though he does not quote the verse. The first words cited—Κρῆτες ἀεὶ ψεῦσται—are quoted by numerous writers, among them St. Paul (Titus 1.12).

²⁶⁷ The premiss that if the tales are lying, their subjects are non-existent does not convince Bardy, who points to the Apocryphal Gospels; but if *all* the accounts are lies, then it does seem reasonable

to doubt the existence of their subjects and that is what Athenagoras has aimed at showing. As he says, it is all or nothing; one cannot pick and choose between tales.

[268] πάθη covers not only their sufferings (such as those of the Titans) but also their yielding to passion (as in the stories of Zeus and Ares).

[269] This closes the argument that is meant to clear the Christians from the charge of atheism; now follows the defence of their moral conduct.

[270] Before Athenagoras, Tatian *Orat.* 25.3, and Justin, 1 *Apol.* 26.7, had alluded to these charges, but Athenagoras is the earliest to deal with them fully. The occasion of the Thyestes charge is quite probably the use by the early Christians of the title ὁ παῖς θεοῦ, the Son of God, for Christ, along with an imperfect understanding of the mystery of the Eucharist. For the Oedipus charge, there was possibly an occasion in the Christian usage of the titles Brother and Sister indiscriminately among themselves and in the practice of the kiss of peace; but there are on record also the stories of Nicholas and the Nicolaites (see Eusebius, *Hist. eccl.* 3.29) and the passage in Clement of Alexandria, *Strom.* 3.4.26 where a tradition of Matthias is quoted for the very ambiguous doctrine that one must abuse the flesh. The behaviour of Simon Magus and Helena may have been counted as Christian by some of the opponents of the new religion. Some historians favour the view that these calumnies were first brought against the Jews by their enemies and by the Jews passed on to the Christians at the time of the burning of Rome (A.D. 64), by way of Poppaea and her Jewish friends.

[271] Pythagoras was said to have perished when one of his lodges was burnt down by his enemies (Diogenes Laertius 8.1.3; Plutarch, *Stoic. rep.* 1051c); but see J. Burnet, *Early Greek Philosophy* (London 1914) 89–92.

[272] Philo, *De vit. cont.* 14, praised Democritus for his disregard of wealth; but no source other than the present is available for the story of his banishment, though that of Heraclitus was generally accepted in antiquity. It could even be inferred from fr. 114 of his works.

[273] Marcus Aurelius himself (*Med.* 6.47) couples Socrates, Pythagoras, and Heraclitus as 'noble philosophers.'

[274] For Socrates the Christians had a feeling of reverence, referring to him in accounts of their own martyrs (e.g. *Acta Apollonii* 41). Athenagoras keeps to a middle course between calling these men Christians before their time (Justin, 1 *Apol.* 46.3) and mocking at them as Tatian did (*Orat.* 25).

[275] ἑκάστου ἡμῶν ἀνος is the reading of the MS, which looks like

the ordinary contraction for ἄνθρωπος; but this is hardly satisfactory. I have supposed the reading to be αἶνος (which Athenagoras could have borrowed from Matt. 21.16 or Luke 18.43, or even 1 Cor. 4.5).

276 The important distinction of 'with God' from 'with God's aid' is certainly demanded by the Greek prepositions. Thus Athenagoras is making clear the strictly supernatural character of the bliss of heaven and setting forth the elements of a famous problem in Christian theology.

277 The husband of Rhea was Kronos and Zeus was their child, but there was some confusion in the legends, and it may have been that Zeus was credited with sons by Rhea. By Kore—his daughter by Demeter—Zeus had a son, Dionysus. In late Hellenistic times there were alphabetical lists of the persons involved in Zeus's promiscuities and philanderings—cf. Roscher 5.581–87.

278 Thyestes, according to the Sophoclean form of the saga, begot Aegisthus by his daughter Pelopia, Apollo having told him that by doing this he might have revenge for his banquet of human flesh (see Servius on *Aen.* 11.262).

279 The text is not easily construed owing to the presence of the word διάφοροι. Schwartz and Geffcken change it to ἀδιάφοροι, which is the Stoic word for the morally indifferent. The sense would then be: 'So far are we from being morally neutral in the matter that we think immodest thoughts sinful.' This is good enough, but as Athenagoras has used ἀδιάφθορος below, it seems reasonable to suppose that he could have written διάφθοροι here, meaning corrupters. (It is odd that, though the compound is a common Greek word, the simple has not been found in use.)

280 The text is from Matt. 5.28.

281 Athenagoras may be thinking of the fable of Gyges's ring which in Plato's *Republic* (359c) is used as an example of the feebleness of human laws without the sanction of public opinion. The Christian idea of justice is not that covered by Plato's definition of 'doing one's job,' but a law of equality, the golden rule of the Sermon on the Mount.

282 There is lacking in the text some noun in the feminine which would define the nature of the νόμος and would supply an antecedent to the feminine relative pronoun. I have translated as if ἰσότης was there, but the gap could be filled in many other ways.

283 The law forbidding the second kiss is not Scriptural, and may come from some early Church Order now lost. Clement, *Paed.* 3.11.81 f. (see also A. Resch, *Agrapha* [2 ed.] 177) has a polemic against the abuse of the kiss. Some, he says, fill the assembly with the

loud smacks of their salutations. The love of God, according to St. John, is that we should keep His commandments, not that we should slobber over each other's lips.

284 There seems to be a gap in the text after the citation of the law, unless, as seems more probable, what follows is also to be regarded as part of the law that is being quoted. I have so translated it.

285 A salutation (προσκύνημα) means literally the kissing of the hand to someone. This was a common pagan practice in the presence of idols (e.g. Apuleius, *Met.* 4.28; cf. K. M. Hofmann, *Philema Hagion* [diss. Erlangen, Gütersloh 1938] 81–83) and is probably as old as the Babylonian empire. From the papyri a phrase like σοῦ προσκυνήσω τὴν χεῖρα (*Berliner griech. Urkunden* 423.15, of the 2nd century A.D.) shows that the meaning of adoration had by now gone from the word. Yet Bardy still clings to this meaning, in spite of its unsuitability to the context.

286 The ethical theory that the purpose of marriage is the begetting of children, and not the pleasure of the contracting parties, was commonly held by the Stoics (cf. Philo, *De Ios.* 43; Musonius, in Stobaeus, *Flor.* 6.61; Plutarch, *Coni. praec.* 144b). Plutarch, *loc. cit.*, says pointedly that a man should not sow where he does not wish to grow a crop: μὴ σπείροντας ἐξ ὧν οὐδὲν αὐτοῖς φύεσθαι θέλουσιν). This analogy with agriculture is used by Philo, *De spec. leg.* 3.32 f., and by the Ps.-Aristotle (fr. 143 Rose). Marcus Aurelius, *Med.* 6.13, 9.1, fully shared these views and would welcome their statement by Athenagoras. For a fuller discussion of the point see K. v. Preysing, 'Ehezweck und zweite Ehe bei Athenagoras' *Theol. Quartalschrift* 110 (1929) 85–110. Though Athenagoras uses this Stoic concept here, he is aware that he is applying it to a new thing, the marriage of Christians. The acknowledgement here that Christians have their own laws on marriage, with its oblique reference to 1 Thess. 4.4, is of great importance as showing that Christianity had already achieved a social organization in spite of the difficulties of persecution; although no apostolic or patristic law of the Church on marriage can be cited prior to the decree of Callistus on the marriage of slaves (Hippolytus, *Ref. haer.* 9.12.24) of about A.D. 220. For the practice of lifelong virginity by Christians there is the contemporary account by the pagan Galen in his celebrated fragment (cf. R. Walzer, *Galen on Jews and Christians* [Oxford 1949] 15). Justin, 1 *Apol.* 15.6, had already made the same claim. In this connexion he used the text of Matt. 19.11 f., as Athenagoras does here. It is unlikely that they took it in the literal sense of physical castration, though elsewhere (1 *Apol.* 29.2) Justin tells of a Christian youth in Egypt who offered to undergo this in order to prove to the

prefect of Egypt that the charges of promiscuity levelled against the Christians were baseless.

287 A word is probably missing here. τὰ ἡμέτερα by itself could signify 'our business.'

288 These hard words on second marriages are quite in sympathy with the Stoic teaching and not really according to Christian practice. One Father of the Church by himself is not a sufficient witness to Catholic doctrine, nor is he personally infallible. Plutarch, *Quaest. om.* 105, said that a first marriage was entirely defensible, but a second was an abomination. He gave this as a reason why Roman widows married at festival-time, when everyone was busy with the festival and they might hope to escape notice, while maidens married outside of festival-time. Jerome, *Adv. Iovin.* 1.49, describes, after Seneca, how the *Flaminica* could never marry when her husband, the *Flamen Dialis*, died, nor could he marry if she died (cf. Ovid, *Fast.* 6.232; Tertullian, *De exhort. cast.* 13, *De monog.* 17=ACW 13.62 and 107, with n. 4 on p. 112; and in general see G. H. Joyce, *Christian Marriage* [2 ed. London 1948] 591 f., for the sequel to this idea in the Greek Church).

289 The citation is from Matt. 19.9, without the well-known exceptive clause. Some have used this fact to support the view that the clause is a non-Matthaean interpolation (see J. MacRory, *The New Testament and Divorce* [London 1934] 69).

290 It is worth noticing that it is any *consummated* marriage which Athenagoras regards as a bar to divorce.

291 The covert adultery of a second marriage when the first wife is dead, does not appear obvious. He might, of course, have appealed to the 'marriage of true minds' which the first union had set up and which could never allow the bereaved husband to admit a second wife to share that mental communing he had enjoyed with the first. Montanists and Novatians took this line and also used the comparison of marriage to the union of Christ and the Church to justify their prohibition of second marriages. In 1 Tim. 3.2, 12, 5.9, and Titus 1.6 the limitation to a single marriage is pronounced a fitting condition for those who are to be priests, deacons, or 'widows.' Even now the Church refuses to give the nuptial blessing twice to the same person.

292 The text is corrupt here. I have translated what is approximately the sense. It may be that a gloss has worked its way into the text, as there are quite too many accusatives.

293 I translate Wilamowitz's correction καὶ τί for the MS ὅτι.

294 The proverb is not otherwise known.

²⁹⁵ Rom. 1.27 is alluded to, but the details show that Athenagoras is not relying on Scripture alone for his denunciation.

²⁹⁶ The beautiful is regarded as a transcendental quality, like truth and goodness, which belong analogously to God and to creatures. No Platonist could have thought otherwise. Cf. Clement, *Protr.* 4.49.2.

²⁹⁷ ποιεῖν or συνειδέναι must be understood with λέγουσιν. Bardy's version, 'ce qu'ils appellent leurs dieux,' is hardly possible. No pagan said that sodomy was a god, though they did say that the gods were guilty of it (e.g. Zeus with Ganymede). It is better to put the comma after ἐπ' αὐτῶν, and I have done this for the translation.

²⁹⁸ The ancients believed that fish were more hasty and violent in copulating than any animal (Aristotle, *De gen. anim.* 718 a 1–10). This mention of fish leads Athenagoras on to speak of the cannibalism of fish, καὶ γάρ indicating the transition. For this cannibalism see Hesiod, *Op.* 277.

²⁹⁹ The translation follows Schwartz's punctuation of the text, where the long parenthesis ends at δίκαις; Bardy and Pratten give entirely different renderings. βιάζεσθαι νόμους is normal Greek, as Pratten saw, but as Bardy did not, creating thus for himself difficulties about laws which the Christians 'were forced to disobey.' The *lex Scantinia* against sodomy (of 50 B.C. or earlier: cf. *Dig.* 47.11.1) had been enforced by Domitian against various senators and equites (cf. Suetonius, *Dom.* 8.3), and it is likely that Athenagoras is referring to this law here. The *Digest* (48.8.4 f.) shows that Hadrian had much ado to put down immorality in the provinces.

³⁰⁰ This Christian duty is expressed in Luke 6.28 f.

³⁰¹ The style becomes more fervid now, and a verb has been dropped from the third sentence of the section, but there is no reason to suppose with Schwartz and Geffcken that it was ever written in the text.

³⁰² Slaves might be tortured to make them give evidence against their Christian masters. It was so often the practice to obtain this evidence by torture for use in court that men who were accused would liberate their slaves to prevent it happening. It is of interest to see that some Christians were rich enough to own slaves.

³⁰³ The text is corrupt. Perhaps ἥττων σπουδῆς περὶ τὰς . . . ἔχει would be the simplest change. This is what I have translated, though Geffcken's conjecture of ἡδυπαθῶν σπουδὰς περὶ . . . is also likely.

³⁰⁴ Educated pagans from Cicero and Seneca onwards began to show distaste for gladiatorial shows and *venationes*, but the populace loved them. They were abolished after the empire had accepted Christianity, in A.D. 325. Imperial shows (*munera*) would obviously be more elaborate than those of an ordinary magistrate.

305 Abortion was condemned by a Jewish philosopher like Philo, *De spec. leg.* 3.108–115, or Josephus, *C. Ap.* 2.202. The Roman law did not directly forbid it, but an extension of the *Lex Cornelia de sicariis et veneficiis* was used against it (cf. *Dig.* 48.8.3.2). It was not murder but an offence against the husband's rights (*Dig.* 47.11.4 and 48.19.39) when the *wife* defrauded him of the child he had a right to expect of her. Seneca, *De cons. ad Helv.* 16.3, and Juvenal, *Sat.* 6.595, speak as if the avoidance of abortion were the nobler course without clearly reprobating its performance. It was really only with the coming of Christianity that the vice was condemned (cf. Conc. Ancyr. *can.* 21 of A.D. 314). The contemporary Council of Neo-Caesarea (*can.* 6) by its legislation on the separate baptizing of pregnant mothers and of their babies when born, established in the Church the idea that the embryo is a human person, against the Roman law idea that the embryo was simply a part of the mother. The *Apocalypsis Petri* (Akhmim fr. 26) and the *Oracula Sibyllina* 2.282, which depend upon it, as also Clement, *Eclog. proph.* 48.1, and Methodius, *Symp.* 2.6, assign a special punishment in hell to those who procure abortion by corrupting the work of God or by accelerating the birth in such a way as to cause the death of the child. *Barnabas* 19.5 and *Didache* 2.2 (cf. ACW 6.62 and 16) give a general prohibition of abortion and the exposure of infants. Clement, *Paed.* 2.10.96.1, is more explicit, condemning the use of 'drugs which slay human progeny begotten according to the Providence of God.' Justin, 1 *Apol.* 27.1, 29.1, and the *Letter to Diognetus* 5.6 (= ACW 6.139), and many others condemn exposure of infants. The pagan who wrote to his wife in the year 1 B.C.: 'If you are delivered of a male child, let it live; if of a female, expose it' (*Oxy. pap.* 4.744), was more frank than many of his contemporaries but not more dissolute. Aristotle thought abortion at an early stage of pregnancy preferable to exposure (*Pol.* 1335 b 25). The *alimenta* so much promoted by Trajan and the 2nd-century administration (see OCD s.v.) were a pagan attempt to meet the evils of exposure. Musonius—cf. Stobaeus, *Flor.* 75.15 and 84.21— was perhaps alone among pagans in condemning abortion and exposure outright. For the best recent summary of the subject, cf. J. H. Waszink, 'Abtreibung,' RAC 1 (1950) 55–60.

306 Athenagoras answers this difficulty himself in his other treatise, which may therefore be regarded as later in date.

307 λῆρος describes just what the Athenians thought about St. Paul in Acts 17.32.

308 Tertullian, *Ad nat.* 1.19, repeats the statement, appealing (§7) to the belief in transmigration or *animarum reciprocatio*. Athenagoras

cannot mean this, but must be thinking of such tales as the raising of
Melissa (Herodotus 5.92) by Periander, or of Orpheus and Eurydice.
Justin, 1 *Apol.* 18.3–5, had already covered this ground, but Athenagoras is probably not following him, as he does not repeat Justin's
argument (*ibid.* 19.1–3) from the strangeness of the contrast between
human semen and a living baby to the possibility of a similar contrast
between a dead body and one that has risen. Philosophers such as
Plutarch, *De ser. num. vind.* 560 f., accept the immortality of the soul,
and do not think (*ibid.* 567c) to differentiate strictly between soul and
body. The old Greek belief that the soul after death was a manikin,
a dwarf resembling the dead man (as shown on the early vase paintings)
would certainly favour this confusion.

[309] Pythagoras, Plato, and Aristotle were credited with the view (cf.
Ps.-Plutarch, *De plac. phil.* 905b) that semen is ἀσώματον and bodiless,
and hence it would make sense for them to say that body is produced
from what is bodiless by some kind of ideal composition.

[310] Pythagoras and Plato are not put forward as saying that the bodily
elements come together again, but Athenagoras is maintaining that
their view allows of this.

[311] This remark suggests that Athenagoras has already in mind his
second treatise and makes one wonder whether after all he was actually
addressing the emperor or not. Richardson (292 f.) takes it for granted
that he did not, and in this view he has P. Keseling 'Athenagoras,'
RAC 1 (1950) 881, to support him. S. Mansel, who wrote the article
on Athenagoras for the DCB, was equally sure that the work reached
the emperor in one form or other, either by being spoken or by presentation as a libellus supplex. The *Acts of Isidore and Lampon* and other
'pagan martyrs,' even if they are not accurate reports of what was
said, show that it was not unusual for the emperors to take personal
cognizance of such matters of justice, and one need not be too sceptical
about the chances of Athenagoras receiving a hearing.

[312] Prayer for the emperor was practised by the Christians according
to teaching of 1 Tim. 2.2 (alluded to here), Rom. 13.1, and 1 Peter
2.13. Among the early Fathers Clement of Rome (61) and Justin,
1 *Apol.* 17.3, speak in favour of it.

[313] That son may follow father would be a graceful compliment to
Commodus.

[314] 1 Tim. 2.2.

THE RESURRECTION

¹ ἐν τούτοις refers back to the opening words παντὶ δόγματι καὶ λόγῳ. Some editors and translators, not seeing this, changed the text to ἐν τοῖς οὖσιν.

² εἱρμός is a Stoic word for a chain of causes or a rapid succession of images.

³ This rather stilted beginning shows the hand of the schoolmaster, accustomed to give lessons in rhetoric.

⁴ The agricultural analogy is Platonic, being frequently used, in conjunction with that drawn from the doings of technicians, to open out a subject, as in *Euthyphro* 2d, 7c.

⁵ The first principles (ὑποθέσεις) are probably to be understood in the Aristotelian sense of an axiom necessarily true and resting upon the nature of God.

⁶ Polycarp (7.1 = ACW 6.79, where see J. A. Kleist's n. 57) said that those who twist the Christian gospel to suit their own lusts and deny the resurrection and judgment are the first-born of Satan. A similar denial of all resurrection for the sake of a life of pleasure seems to be regarded here.

⁷ Structure (σύστασις) is a Platonic term for the constitution or *Gestalt* of a thing; cf. *Tim.* 32c, 36d, etc.

⁸ Marcus Aurelius (*Med.* 4.32) held the view of dissolution here taken for granted, that the elements of the human body, when released from the bodily structure by death, went to join a common stock.

⁹ Following Plato (*Phil.* 25e and *Theaet.* 159c), where ἐφ'ἑκάστων means 'on each of several occasions,' I take ἐφ'ἑτέρων here to be a similar phrase. Pratten's version: 'the judgment we form of other matters,' seems an irrelevant remark for Athenagoras to have made.

¹⁰ Man did not come into being at the first creation. This is clear from Gen. 1.27, see also the Platonic philosophy (*Tim.* 39e) which said the world at the birth of time did not yet contain the living creatures that were to come into being within it.

¹¹ Schwartz reads παρ'αὐτοῖς while the manuscript A has αὐτῆς. The reference of αὐτοῖς would be to the philosophers whose views on the origin of the constituents of the human body, whether from a common matter, or from ultimate and irreducible elements or from seed, have just been cited. Anaximander favoured the idea of an origin

from a common matter or slime, Anaxagoras (and later, the doctor Asclepiades) an origin from irreductible elements, while Galen seems to have been content with the idea of an origin from seed (*Nat. fac.* 1.6).

12 A minor MS, Parisinus 450, has been followed here for its reading πλήθει. Schwartz reads πλήθη with A, and then, though he adds the word εἰς to the text, he says, 'ἀγείρειν κόρον *non intellego.*'

13 St. Thomas (*IV Sent.* 44.1.2.1 and *Suppl.* 80.4 ad 1) discusses the objections raised in this section, though without coming to any final decision on the merits of various alternative answers to them. See further, A. Michel, 'Resurrection,' DTC 13.2 (1937) 2555 ff.

14 The Medic banquet may be some grisly story of cannibalism among the Medes such as the story of Harpagus (Herodotus 1.119), but it is just possibly a reference to what Medea contrived when she persuaded the daughters of Pelias to boil him with herbs (Pindar, *Pyth.* 4.250) in the hope of rejuvenating him. For Thyestes, see n. 278 above.

15 I have followed J. D. Denniston, *The Greek Particles* (Oxford 1934) 282, in dealing with ἤ πού γε in this a fortiori argument. From the examples there given, it would seem that Plato preferred to put the inference first and to follow up with a simple statement, an order that Athenagoras does not adopt.

16 Galen (*Nat. fac.* 1.10 f.) describes in considerable detail the digestive process in man. Emulsion (χυλός) is brought from the digestive system by the portal vessel; reaches the liver and is there transformed into pneuma or natural spirit, which is the sustenance of the vital principle.

17 The three cleansings and dissolutions are either presentation, adhesion, and assimilation, as Galen describes them—*op. cit.* 3.13.200—or, more exactly, cooking, ingesting, emulsification (πέψις, ἀνάδοσις, χύλωσις) as described *ibid.* 2.8.111 f.

18 The natural process of straining (or drawing off the moisture from food that has been ingested) is described by Galen (*op. cit.* 1.15.58) who compares the action of the kidneys to that of wicker strainers (τάλαρος) into which the curdled milk is thrown during cheesemaking.

19 The 'excessive mass' or filling supposes ἐπεισαχθέντα, which is the correction in MS a for the reading ἐπεισχυθει . . . τα of A. Yet ἐπεισχέω does exist and may have been used here.

20 The action of stronger and weaker elements in digestion is very like the interplay of rival forms in Plato's *Phaedo* (102d–106e). Galen (*op. cit.* 1.10.22) has the same metaphor explaining why it is that meat is more nourishing for men than radishes.

21 The conversion of food into humours or juices (χυμοί) was held by Galen to be the work of many organs. Blood had to be thickened in order to become flesh; for conversion into bone, it had to be thickened, hardened, and whitened. Presentation and adhesion go before complete assimilation, as in n. 17 above.

22 The resurrection of the humours in the body is discussed by St. Thomas (*IV Sent*. 44.1.2.3, *ad* 2). He holds that they will be in the risen body, even though not used in heaven. In this he is influenced by Augustine's famous reply (*Serm*. 243.7: ML 38.1146) to one who asked if risen bodies will have sexual organs, since in heaven there is no marrying or giving in marriage: in his reply Augustine cites the parallel of beards in this life, adding: *Speciem video; usum non quaero*. It is surprising to find Athenagoras, so early in the history of Christian theology, descending to such details. His attempt to harmonize theology and the medical science of his day (and of every other day down to 1900) is noteworthy.

23 The soft fat (δημῶν) does not seem wanted here, and Wilamowitz has bracketed the word, but the genitive absolute seems thrown in at the end of the sentence as an afterthought, having no causal connexion with what has gone before. Avoiding this easy way out, I have tried to make sense of the text as it stands. The flesh and soft fat could be the incoming meat, while the fat membranes are those of the eater. The idea of storage is found in Galen (*op. cit*. 1.10.23) who speaks of a receptacle where superfluities are stored until they reach the quantum necessary for discharge.

24 Pratten misconstrues this to mean: 'We are very well aware that some brutes have human forms.' Apart from grammar, it is clear that Athenagoras cannot mean that. His reference to the daring of the poets would then be pointless. Pratten may have been subconsciously influenced by the Darwinism of his day, but Athenagoras is far from such ideas. He is simply concerned—in passing—to show that he is aware of the difficulty against his theory of natural foods that might be caused by the existence of a half-human monster; it would then be true that human bodies never become the flesh of other human beings who feed upon them, and yet this half-human monster might succeed in assimilating human flesh as the Titans were thought to have done (cf. E. Wüst, 'Titanes,' RE 6A2 [1937] 1491–1508).

25 If cannibalism is against nature, then there is some basis in nature for Athenagoras's doctrine of natural foods. God can be supposed to have laid down for man at least some negative food laws. Herodotus (4.18.3) spoke of ἀνδροφάγοι who lived beyond the Scythians in S. Russia. In 4.106 he makes them nomads of Scythian garb but not of

Scythian speech. All Greeks felt curiosity about the existence of such creatures, as they might be held to prove the conventional character of most human laws.

26 The parallel with the potter or carpenter is a by-product of the argument from design, but not a natural one. God has the perfections which we can observe in human nature but without the attendant imperfections. If we ask whether God has a sense of humour, the answer is that he can appreciate far better than we can the neatness or fitness of a humorous saying or episode, but he cannot share in our surprise (the second element in our enjoyment of a joke), for nothing is concealed from Him.

27 The word 'probable' (ἔνδοξος) is from Aristotle, who defines it (*Top.* 100a.30 Bekker) as what is judged by everyone, or by the *maior et sanior pars*, to be true.

28 The supposition of animals surviving in the next world is put in the most remote form possible to syntax. Perhaps Athenagoras was disinclined to rule out as completely impossible this element from the Pythagorean doctrine of transmigration of souls while rejecting the chief heads of that doctrine.

29 The natural servitude of animals to man implies by contrast in the mind of Athenagoras that the servitude of man to man is not natural.

30 Pratten renders: 'And besides, with creatures that have no notion of justice, there can be no complaint of injustice,' suggesting a causal connexion absent from the Greek. Athenagoras is not saying that one can never wrong a being that is itself without understanding of right and wrong. The οὐδέ makes it clear that his argument is an a fortiori: 'Man's resurrection will not wrong animals that are his servants here. But they are the only beings it might be thought to injure (and as they have no sense of right and wrong and cannot complain, someone else must do it for them). Ergo man's resurrection will injure no one.' The relative clause is not giving the reason why animals are not wronged, but is an aside to explain why the argument has taken this form.

31 At this point the text fails us. MS A has undergone correction and erasure, and there has certainly been a telescoping of the argument. By his scheme for this chapter Athenagoras has now to show two points: that the body is not wronged by being raised from the dead, and that it is not a work unworthy of God to raise up a dead body. He tackles (1) by saying: 'If now, when it, a corruptible thing, is associated with an incorruptible soul, ⟨God has not wronged the body, how can the union of immortal body with immortal soul⟩ be wrong?'

He will answer (2) by an argument a fortiori : 'If God has condescended to create a lowly mortal body, surely He can be expected to produce one that is glorious and immortal.' The οὐ μὴν οὐδέ after the lacuna shows that a new point is being made (cf. Denniston, *op. cit.* 338). Hence the first part of the argument is incomplete as the text stands, and some words expressing what I have here put within brackets must be supplied.

[32] The go-between or informer was generally an object of scorn in Greece, but the word can bear a good sense (cf. Lysias 12.32).

[33] The gradual corruption consists in the poorer quality of such after-grass by comparison with the original crop. The idea of a second *sowing* is not necessarily implied by ἐπισπορά.

[34] This summarizes the argument of the rest of the book.

[35] *Agens agit propter finem*, as applied to natural agents at least, was accepted as an axiom by the Stoics from whom Athenagoras has probably derived it. The phrase he uses, κοινότερον σκοποῦντες, suggests that this is one of the Stoic κοιναὶ ἔννοιαι. For the extension of the axiom from intellectual creatures to all other living beings, see St. Thomas, *Summa c. gent.* 3.2.

[36] The description of the motive for creative activity is given in general terms, which would suit artistic creation as well as the begetting of children, though from the example that follows it is clearly the latter which Athenagoras has chiefly in mind.

[37] The evident decay of senatorial families in the Rome of the 1st century A.D. shows that this motive of procuring a vicarious immortality did not count for much in the educated pagan mind, though even there a desire to perpetuate the family name by the adoption of a son was commonly shown by childless couples.

[38] To play the immortal as far as one may is Aristotle's advice to the sage (*Eth. Nic.* 1177b.33 Bywater) where this same word ἀθανατίζειν occurs, of which Athenagoras is using the compound form.

[39] Athenagoras, while accepting the fact that men are not equal (by his grouping them into higher and lower degrees), is emphatic in his rejection of the first principle of slavery enunciated by Aristotle in his dictum that slaves are animated tools (*Eth. Nic.* 1161b.4 Bywater).

[40] A sane attitude to slavery seems to go with a lack of sentimentality about the rights of animals, as here.

[41] The end of creation as the manifestation of God's perfection in the good things He imparts to creatures, as the Vatican Council defined (Denz. 1783), is here for the first time clearly expressed in Christian thought. Theophilus of Antioch (2.10) is later in date and much more

vague. For the Scholastic development of this idea, see J. Stufler: *Why God Created the World* (tr. by E. F. Sutcliffe, Stanbrook 1937).

[42] This image of God is in man's nature, and is not something conferred upon him by grace or at baptism. Athenagoras is more precise in his thinking than some of the Greek Fathers who talk loosely about grace restoring in man the image of God defaced by Adam's sin. The full statement of the doctrine is that of Irenaeus, *Adv. haer.* 5.6.1 H.

[43] The argument for the perpetual endurance in being of the human soul is here put in the form that was to become traditional in Christian schools. The cause is 'comprehended within the nature and regarded only in the aspect of one that exists,' in the sense that God, man's cause, *is* Being, and that Being is related by a profound and intrinsic analogy to the being that man is said to have, so that the two propositions: God exists, and: Man exists, are both true, and to some extent true in the same sense, even though one could not generalize from them and say: Existence is what God and man have, for that would be to make existence a common predicate, which it is not.

If *x* is God, He exists, is true and an analytic proposition.
If *x* is a man, he exists, is neither.

The phenomena of this existential predication have not been attended to by Logical Positivism, but they provide an instance where one proposition is analytic and an exactly similar one is in need of verification. Existence enters into the concept of God, for His nature is to exist, and it is ascertainable of men in particular, though not entering into the concept of man. Yet, when man is known to exist (when the mind reflects upon its own experience, or argues by a cumulative process to the existence of other minds like its own), his existence is seen—precisely because man is in the image of God—to be related by analogy to the existence of God. Where there is no such image—as in animals, trees, or plants—*there* can be found no such analogy, and hence no reason for their exemption from annihilation. In his few pregnant words here Athenagoras has foreseen all that is true in the philosophy of existentialism.

[44] The image of God in the human soul is not a static thing like a stamp on wax, but a developing or growth towards a pattern of existence. A man is more himself the more like he is to God, and God, having imparted to him that tendency to 'become himself' or to win his soul, cannot be supposed out of contrariness to will that such a tendency should be suddenly arrested by annihilation. On these two considerations does Athenagoras base his argument by these two vital and carefully chosen phrases.

⁴⁵ This carries the argument a stage further, on to less sure ground. Body and soul, two incomplete but mutually supporting realities in man, each pay their share of tribute (εἰσφορά) to the common stock of existence. The soul has a function with regard to the body—that of driver (ἐπιστάτης) or commander—so that if the soul alone survive, it will be somehow incomplete in its new existence. The body is a being of change; its law is to be ever in flux. Athenagoras does not produce reasons for stating why this law of bodily existence tends in the limit to a state of μεταβολή πρὸς τὸ κρεῖττον, to a final change for the better, and here his argument is halting. Later theologians were to argue that the resurrection of the body cannot be proved by philosophical reasoning. To say that it can, is to fall into Origen's phantasy of the spherical bodies of the risen (*De princ.* 2.10.2 and Denz. 207). That would be a change for the better with a vengeance.

⁴⁶ The phrase is echoed in Alciphron (3.5.3), but as his date is probably slightly later than Athenagoras's, he must be regarded as the less original.

⁴⁷ This repeats the argument of n. 45 above in a more rhetorical form. If one asked: How do you know God would not create the being you describe and then annihilate it? the answer would be: Of course, God *could* annihilate it, but given what we know of the wisdom of God and of the *dynamic* nature of this image of Him by which man tends to return Godwards, the idea is really self-contradictory.

⁴⁸ The insistence that man must have his body with him for ever implies in Athenagoras a view of man that is not quite Platonic. If man *as man* is incomplete without his body, that body is not a prison or tomb (as in Pythagorean and Platonic thought) and its union with the soul is a good thing. Athenagoras does not develop this thought, but it is essential for his argument. He would have to say that it is a good thing for the body to have a soul as rider, just as it is good for a horse to be ridden.

⁴⁹ The idea of strict logical sequence, καθ᾽εἰρμόν, is Stoic, being used by M. Aurelius (3.4 and 12.23), not in complete contrast with natural succession, but to express a further refinement of the idea of nature. Ἑιμαρμένη, or the orderly procession of Destiny, is the root idea from which εἰρμός is derived by Alexander of Aphrodisias (*De an.* 2): cf. Cicero, *De divin.* 1.55.125. The chain of reasoning is then set down to provide a summary of the remaining chapters.

⁵⁰ This repeats the distinction of the previous note between φύσις and εἰρμός. The κοιναὶ καὶ φυσικαὶ ἔννοιαι of the Stoics are axioms or first principles of nature which are incapable of demonstration. The

conclusions produced from them are produced by εἱρμός, or strict logical sequence.

⁵¹ Axioms cannot be demonstrated to a beginner or to an opponent. One can only present them to him and ask him to see them for himself. Athenagoras suggests that all men *will* see them if their memory of such axioms (or, as we might say, their half-conscious awareness of them) is clarified. One cannot be sure from the language that Athenagoras is here using the Platonic theory of reminiscence: ὑπόμνησις is not a technical word.

⁵² The distinction between truth and its guarantee (ἀλήθεια and ἀσφάλεια) is not exactly that between the objective truth of things and the subjective certainty of our state of mind about them, as Pratten renders it. Rather should one say that the guarantee of the truth is the orderliness of the process by which it is derived from the axioms—and this orderliness is not simply a subjective state of mind.

⁵³ Athenagoras may have been following the Western text of 1 Cor. 15.51, which reads: *We shall all rise again, but we shall not all be changed.* His idea that all shall rise but not all be judged, is certainly singular. He has cited 1 Cor. 15.53 here in ch. 18, and must therefore have known this passage.

⁵⁴ The universality of the Judgment is asserted by the Second Council of Lyons in 1274 (Denz. 464). As this decree speaks of all men having to appear before the tribunal of Christ to render an account of their *deeds,* it is doubtful whether the Council should be held to include those who die in infancy. In any case Athenagoras is much ahead of his time in speculating about these things at all.

⁵⁵ The 'class of derived beings' is represented in the text by εἱρμός. This sense, somewhat removed from the meaning of 'a logical series of deductions,' occurs again in chs. 17 and 24, and represents an extended use of logical terms for concrete realities. All philosophers from time to time indulge in this habit of extension, according to the general principle, *Leges mentis, leges entis sunt,* a principle which has led many astray.

⁵⁶ I have borrowed the term 'ingression' from Whitehead to render the phrase κατὰ τὴν ἰδιάζουσαν ἕνωσιν. The individual manner each part has of entering into union with the other parts is what is meant, and we seem otherwise to lack a term to express this.

⁵⁷ The vital premiss in Athenagoras's argument is this statement that it is man who receives ideas. I think a modern Scholastic would say that the body is not a contributory cause to abstract thought, but a condition that can be dispensed with; for sensitive awareness the body *is* a contributory cause, but whether such sensitive awareness will

always be man's destiny, no man could tell without revelation or a *petitio principii* in his argument.

⁵⁸ The soul has been attuned to the needs of the body when it begins to devise rational means for the satisfying of instincts such as the use of fire to prepare the food that will satisfy bodily hunger. It is attuned to the body's experience when it judges of sense data, recalls them, or runs them together in rationally chosen combinations.

⁵⁹ The phrase is ambiguous. One cannot be sure if Athenagoras means that men put the beauty there or that someone put it there for men.

⁶⁰ Permanence is analogously predicated, when applied to God and to man. Hence the Neo-Platonic tendency to speak of God as super-immense, more-than-permanent, and so on: cf. Proclus, *Elem. theol.* prop. 115.

⁶¹ All spiritual natures such as souls are simply permanent. A body that dies and rises again is permanent in a somewhat Pickwickian sense.

⁶² I do not follow Schwartz in supposing a lacuna in the text here. All that is needed is the particle ἤ.

⁶²ᵃ The repetition here of ideas that have appeared in the *Embassy* (see n. 79 to that work) is a sign, if one be needed, that the same author is at work in both treatises. Against recent suggestions that the *Resurrection* comes from a later time and a different author one has to set its remarkable fitness for the intellectual climate of the late 2nd century. The parallels with Galen, Albinus, and Lucian noted here (see nn. 16–18 above and 70, 80, 82 below for examples) are best explained by supposing that the writer is their contemporary. In addition it is to be remembered that with two contemporary Christian writers, Tatian and Theophilus of Antioch, denying the natural immortality of the soul, there was an evident need for an old Platonist such as Athenagoras to write a work that would go beyond the *Phaedo* of his master by bringing in the Christian idea of immortality for the soul and resurrection for the body. For a recent treatment of early Christian ideas about death, see J. A. Fischer, *Studien zum Todesgedanken in der alten Kirche* 1 (Munich 1954); for the present passage, *ibid.* 160 f.

⁶³ Plato (*Rep.* 509b) uses ἐπέκεινα with a genitive to express what is somehow transcendent. The Neo-Platonists use it habitually when describing the analogous knowledge of God. Here the usage is halfway between the two.

⁶⁴ The adjective used is the ὁμοιομερής of Anaxagoras, the term used for the exactly similar particles that make up a natural substance. These were not atoms, for they varied from one natural substance to

another, but would resemble molecules if these could be imagined to be indivisible.

⁶⁵ I have supposed that ἤ might be omitted here, rather than accept Schwartz's emended text.

⁶⁶ This seems to be an argument from uniformity in nature making possible prediction beyond the present scope of the evidence. Thus: This child's smooth skin will harden, wrinkle, shrivel, and die; the same train of events has been observed before, and here is another instance of its beginning.

⁶⁷ The first three stages of man's development—birth, growth, perfection—correspond to those in Irenaeus (*Adv. haer.* 4.63.2 H), but Irenaeus adds other stages, waxing fat, being strengthened, being glorified; and he is really dealing with spiritual growth rather than ὑφεσις and διάλυσις as here. In fact, Irenaeus seems to be transposing to the spiritual plane some list such as that used by Athenagoras here.

⁶⁸ The a fortiori seems to be this: reasoning has proved the resurrection of the body by argument from man's nature and development. Reasoning surpasses experience, and even experience can give us the possibility of sure prediction in spite of appearances. Much more then can reason do so.

⁶⁹ This might be a flash back to Plato's *Republic* (cf. 369b).

⁷⁰ The συναμφότερον is the *compositum* of later Scholastic philosophy. Athenagoras is the first Christian thinker to use the term. It is found in Albinus, *Epit.* 23.3.

⁷¹ Reason is entirely subjugated by passion in the sins of the flesh and can be regarded as being out of action while they are being committed (St. Thomas, 2a–2ae.156.3 ad 1, and art. 4c), but reason must have allowed them to begin, and hence it is only partially true that the soul is without engagement (ἀπροσπαθής) in such sins. This weakens the argument of Athenagoras, who is following Plato here (*Tim.* 86c-e). The term ἀπροσπαθής seems to be of Athenagoras's own coinage. Clement of Alexandria, his disciple, uses it frequently.

⁷² The allusions are to 1 Cor. 15.53 and 2 Cor. 5.10.

⁷³ Plato (*Laws* 899d) admitted a providence. See Armstrong, *op. cit.* 62.

⁷⁴ The pagan point of view—*deorum iniurias dis curae esse*—was that the gods did not really care about men and that the only use of worship and cult activities was that thus one gained a (magical) hold upon the (possibly minor) functioning of divine power. The suggestion in Aristophanes's *Aves*, that the gods will be affected by stopping sacrifices to them on earth, was revolutionary only in its immediate proposal, not in its general assumptions.

⁷⁵ If there is to be no ideal of justice, men are left with the horrors of Orwell's *Animal Farm*.

⁷⁶ This creed is reprehended in Isa. 22.13 and 1 Cor. 15.32. Athenagoras is probably following St. Paul here.

⁷⁷ This was the endless drunken fit which Socrates rejected in the *Apology* of Plato (40c).

⁷⁸ The verb is not in the text; hence Wilamowitz and Schwartz have postulated a lacuna, but in such a declamatory passage the verb 'to be' could very easily be omitted for rhetorical effect.

⁷⁹ The argument from the inadequacy of the sanctions for the moral law in this life to the certainty of some sanction or other in the next is common in Christian ethics, but it is not generally held that such a rational argument proves the need of *bodily* sanctions in the next life.

⁸⁰ The same sorry farce will be played over again. The word ἐπεισκυκλεῖν is very rare, but is a favourite with Lucian, whom therefore Athenagoras may have read. It recalls the εἰσκύκλημα or stage device for withdrawing on a platform the bodies of the dead after they have been rolled out on the ἐκκύκλημα to be shown to the spectators of a tragedy. Greek convention disliked showing the actual murders.

⁸¹ The argument depends upon the assumption that God's idea of justice is like ours and that He will visit spiritual sins upon the soul and fleshly sins upon the flesh. This is no more than a likely guess, for while it must be that God is just, the manner of His exacting punishment cannot be so nearly foretold by reason alone. Athenagoras in the next chapter argues that it can.

⁸² The warfare between body and soul (well described in Francis Thompson's *Health and Holiness* and in many spiritual writers) is here dealt with in close and accurate detail. The tactics of the body are variously described as συναρπαγὴ καὶ κλοπή (seizure and robbery), as ὁλκὴ βιαιοτέρα (abduction by main force), and as συνδρομή (collusion). This last is the term used in Ps.-Aristotle (*Hist. anim.* 636b.13) for the mutual fitness of husband and wife for each other in the work of generation. The terms συναρπαγὴ καὶ κλοπή are found combined in a 2nd-century papyrus (C. Wessely, *Stud. Pal.* 22.177.30) and must have been current as legal jargon.

⁸³ It is not by commission but by omission (of the requisite control) that the soul shares in these fleshly sins; hence it deserves punishment for them, and the argument is not conclusive.

⁸⁴ The words ὅσαι κατὰ τὸν βίον πράξεις may be a generalization for all the activities of one's life, but I incline to view it as a specific term, and I have so translated it.

85 πρωτοπαθεῖν is a medical term used by Galen, meaning usually 'to be principally affected,' but here temporal priority is clearly intended.

86 The question whether the passions are essentially spiritual by nature, or just bodily, or belonging to the *compositum*, was much debated in the proto-Renaissance of the 12th century, though in entire ignorance of this work of Athenagoras. There were Platonists among the medieval Scholastics such as Robert Pullen, and the Neo-Platonism accessible in such works as the Pseudo-Dionysius or the *De Isaac seu de anima* of St. Ambrose, would also tend to distract men from a complete acceptance of the Aristotelian theory of the *compositum*.

87 'Equality of deserts': the distinction here made between a reward merited *de condigno*, or by strict justice, and one merited *de congruo*, or on some proportionate scale, was much developed by later theologians. The root of the matter is in Aristotle who (*Eth. Nic.* 1132b.33 Bywater) has the terms κατ᾿ ἰσότητα and κατ᾿ ἀναλογίαν.

88 The separate souls in Purgatory give honour to God though they cannot practise the four cardinal virtues. Their wills are conformed to the will of God, not by an active and meritorious effort to bring them into conformity, but by a passive acquiescence somewhat akin to the passive state of contemplation.

89 The infinitive χρῆσθαι seems to be used as a proper passive and not as a deponent. Such usage is not without parallel.

90 Ἰδιοπραγία was in Plato a bad thing (*Laws* 875b), akin to selfishness, idiosyncrasy, and the like. But in the course of time it came to have a good connotation, as here. In Plato's discussion, justice is doing one's job (τὰ αὑτοῦ πράττειν or οἰκειοπραγία, *Rep.* 434c), and thus for each part of an organism to fulfil its function, or to engage in its private enterprise, would be an exercise of justice. When the soul has no organic parts under its control, there can be none of this.

91 Cf. Exod. 20.12 f. (Sept.) and Luke 18.20.

92 Plato would agree that there are no differences of sex in souls (*Tim.* 91a).

93 This is the first mention of an audience physically present to Athenagoras as he discourses.

94 The appeal is therefore to an axiom, one of the κοιναὶ ἔννοιαι of the Stoics.

95 The use of the agricultural analogy, on the Platonic model, has been noted above, n.4.

96 Nomos belongs to Physis. Thus did the Stoics resolve the old Greek dilemma of: Either accept law that is mere convention, or the natural state of wildness, but not both together.

97 Lack of disturbance (ἀταραξία) was the goal of human endeavour

tor the Epicureans. This would be no better than the everlasting drunkenness rejected earlier. It is significant that Athenagoras never uses the word.

98 Athenagoras is quite certain that animals have no feeling. Modern psychology has elaborated the rather elementary concepts of emotional life common in Scholastic philosophy, and it would be more correct to say in modern terms that animals have no sentiments. (For the distinction between emotions and sentiments, see F. M. Shand, *Foundations of Character* [2 ed. London 1921].) One might also say that they have no self-regarding emotions, though something like the physical fear of man is experienced by at least the higher animals when in presence of an unresolved and threatening situation.

99 The *natural* end of man was not much in the thoughts of the Fathers or the Scholastic theologians until St. Thomas, trying to make the best and most Christian use of Aristotle's ethical system with its denial of immortality, came to reshape it, towards the end of his life, in his *Commentarii super libros Ethicorum Aristotelis* (ab. 1270). He added to Aristotle the idea of a natural happiness for man in the unending existence of the soul. I have discussed this in a paper read at the Academy of St. Thomas in Rome in 1950 and published among the *Acta Congressus Thomistici*, 1950. With Thomas there is no question of a philosophical proof that the body will share this natural happiness.

100 The argument that unless this man rises again with this soul and this body he is not the same man, would be met by a later theologian with the distinction between principal and accessory. In the soul principally consists the self-identity of this man, and if that survive, he is in the main the same man. His soul will always have a hankering after its own body, and the only question is, revelation apart, to decide how God will counteract that longing so as to make the man happy in heaven. Will He appease it by restoring the body, or in some better way? Reason cannot say for certain.

101 Athenagoras will have nothing to do with reincarnation of the soul in another body, however much the Pythagorean-Platonist tradition held to it.

102 The term for perpetual companionship (συνδιαιωνίζειν) is borrowed from Philo (*De praem. et poen.* 70, *De vit. Mos.* 2.108, etc.); as Philo never uses it with personal objects, the ambiguous τούτοις here is probably to be taken as neuter.

103 I read δόντος with Schwartz and A; older editors had printed ὄντος from some of the minor MSS, meaning 'vision of the one who is.' That would be an easy sense, but I prefer to think that Athenagoras wrote 'vision of the One who gives us that vision.'

[104] It is notable that Athenagoras does not fall into the trap for the unwary (which has caught Dr. Coulton and many another) by arguing that if the blessed are perfectly happy in heaven and if they know of those who are being punished in hell, they must have that knowledge as part of their happiness.

[105] Athenagoras's words are rather obscure. He probably means that the rewards and punishments are so much each man's peculiar affair that he has no intention of concerning himself with others. This does not mean that he denied a general judgment, but that he did believe in a particular one.

INDEX

INDEX

Abdera, 72
abortion, 167
Achatius, *Acts* of, 149
Achilles, 149
Admetus, 55, 149
Adrasteia, 123
adultery, 9, 73, 74
Aegisthus, 163
Aeneas, 149
Aeschylus, 148
    Suppl., 159; *frag.* 350: 56, 149
Aethlius, 142
Aetius, 129 f.
Agamemnon, 29, 124
Agapius, 133
Agraulos, 29, 124
Aidoneus, 56
Albinus, 177
    Epit. 15.1: 140; 15.2: 156; 23.3: 178
Alciphron, *Epist.* 3.5.3: 175
Alcman, 139
Alcmene, 132
Alexander of Abonuteichos, 65 f., 157 f.
Alexander of Aphrodisias, *De an.* 2: 175
Alexander of Jerusalem, *Epist. ad Orig.*, 5, 120
Alexander, otherwise Paris, 65, 157
Alexander the Great, 67 f., 158
Alexandria, catechetical school at, 4–6, 8
Amasis, 66, 157
Amathus, 44, 139
Amore, A., 130
Amphiaraus, 69, 160
analogy of being, 17, 97, 139 f., 174
Anaxagoras, 148, 170, 177
Anaximander, 169
Angelion, 48, 143
angels, 19, 41, 62 f., 91, 134, 153 f.
Anon. *de mundo* 398 a 2: 141; 399 a 14: 140
Antinous, 5, 70, 161

Antoninus Pius, 4 f., 161
Aphrodite, 48, 53, 55, 57, 143, 149, 150
ἀποκατάστασις, 146
Apollo, 44, 48, 56, 67, 138, 143, 149, 151, 163
Apollodorus, 68, 159
Apollonius the martyr, 3, 121
    Acts of, 8: 121; 41: 162
Apollonius Rhodius, *Argon.*, 2. 510: 138
ἀπόρροια, 22 f., 40, 61, 121, 133 f.
Apostolic Constitutions 8.12.16: 24, 121, 137
Apuleius, *Met.* 4.28: 164
Arcadia, 138
Arendzen, J. P., 9
Ares, 54, 149 f., 162
Arethas, 120
Arges, 50
Argos, 48, 160
argument from design, 34, 45, 51, 90, 172
Arianism, 121, 133
Aristaeus, 44, 138
Aristides, *Apol.* 1: 5; 10.5: 160; 12.6: 125
Aristophanes, *Aves*, 151, 178; 690: 145; 1073: 127; *Lys.* 439: 124; *Nub.* 830: 127
Aristotle, 35 f., 46, 129 f., 135, 138, 146, 168
    De caelo 301 a 15: 126; *De gen. anim.* 718 a 1: 166; *De part. anim.* 641 b 19: 64, 155; *Eth. Nic.* 1132 b 33: 180; 1161 b 4: 173; 1177 b 33: 173; *Hist. anim.* 576 a 17: 126; 630 f.: 126; 636 b 13: 179; *Pol.* 1335 b 25: 167; *Top.* 100 a 30: 172
Armstrong, A. H., 146, 150, 158, 178
Artemis, 48, 65, 67, 124, 142 f., 151, 156
Asclepiades, 170
Asclepius, 48, 69 f., 157, 160
Atargatis, *see* Derceto

185

13

ANCIENT CHRISTIAN WRITERS

The Works of the Fathers in Translation

Edited by

J. QUASTEN, S.T.D., and J. C. PLUMPE, Ph.D.